PRAISE FOR THE P

ALL THE WAYS TO SAY I LOVE

"Compelling . . . a bleak vision redole

—Max McGuinness, *Financial Times*

"LaBute's hour-long monologue is haunting . . . To say more is to spoil his perfect ending." —**David Finkle**, *Huffington Post*

"A creeping primal darkness ensnares us in what appears to be an ordinary life." —**Linda Winer**, *Newsday*

"Beware of any mentions of *Reasons to be Happy* in Neil LaBute's dark new play . . . a wrenching solo monologue . . . unsettling to the haunting, heartrending end." —**Jennifer Farrar**, Associated Press

"A densely plotted sonata . . . a portrait of a woman reckoning, without apology or deflection, with a decision that has defined her life." —**Jason Fitzgerald**, *The Village Voice*

THE WAY WE GET BY

"It's sexy, it's starry . . . dangerously irresistible." —**Ben Brantley**, *New York Times*

"*The Way We Get By* has an unexpected sweetness, along with a twist." —**Jennifer Farrar**, Associated Press

"*The Way We Get By* feels like a refreshingly sunnier and more hopeful LaBute, with moments that feel suspiciously like giddy joy." —**Sara Vilkomerson**, *Entertainment Weekly*

"Viscerally romantic, almost shockingly sensitive, even, dare we say it, sweet . . . LaBute . . . dares here to explore less obviously explosive territory. Yet, somehow, this daring feels deep." —**Linda Winer**, *Newsday*

THE MONEY SHOT

"A wickedly funny new comedy." —**Jennifer Farrar**, Associated Press

"An acid-tongued showbiz satire." —**Scott Foundas**, *Variety*

"Fresh, joyously impolite . . . a good and mean little farce." —**Linda Winer**, *Newsday*

"100 minutes of rapid-fire bursts of raucous laughter." —**Michael Dale**, *BroadwayWorld*

"Packs a stunning amount of intelligence into 100 minutes of delectable idiocy."
—**Hayley Levitt**, *TheaterMania*

"Consistently entertaining . . . To his credit, LaBute does not aim for the obvious metaphor: in showbiz, everyone gets screwed. He is more concerned with amusing us." —**Brendan Lemon**, *Financial Times*

REASONS TO BE HAPPY

"Mr. LaBute is more relaxed as a playwright than he's ever been. He is clearly having a good time revisiting old friends . . . you're likely to feel the same way . . . the most winning romantic comedy of the summer, replete with love talk, LaBute-style, which isn't so far from hate talk . . ."
—**Ben Brantley**, *New York Times*

"These working-class characters are in fine, foul-mouthed voice, thanks to the scribe's astonishing command of the sharp side of the mother tongue. But this time the women stand up for themselves and give as good as they get."
—**Marilyn Stasio**, *Variety*

"LaBute has a keen ear for conversational dialogue in all its profane, funny and inelegant glory." —**Joe Dziemianowicz**, *New York Daily News*

"LaBute . . . nails the bad faith, the grasping at straws, the defensive barbs that mark a tasty brawl." —**Elisabeth Vincentelli**, *New York Post*

"Intense, funny, and touching . . . In following up with the lives of his earlier characters, LaBute presents another compassionate examination of the ways people struggle to connect and try to find happiness."
—**Jennifer Farrar**, Associated Press

"Terrifically entertaining." —**Philip Boroff**, *Bloomberg*

"A triumph . . . always electric with life. LaBute has a terrific way of demonstrating that even in their direst spoken punches . . . fighting lovers are hilarious. . . . completely convincing." —**David Finkle**, *Huffington Post*

REASONS TO BE PRETTY

"Mr. LaBute is writing some of the freshest and most illuminating American dialogue to be heard anywhere these days . . . *Reasons* flows with the compelling naturalness of overheard conversation. . . . It's never easy to say what you mean, or to know what you mean to begin with. With a delicacy that belies its crude vocabulary, *Reasons to be Pretty* celebrates the everyday heroism in the struggle to find out." —**Ben Brantley**, *New York Times*

"There is no doubt that LaBute knows how to hold an audience. . . . LaBute proves just as interesting writing about human decency as when he is writing about the darker urgings of the human heart." —**Charles Spencer**, *Telegraph*

"Funny, daring, thought-provoking . . ."   —**Sarah Hemming**, *Financial Times*

IN A DARK DARK HOUSE

"Refreshingly reminds us . . . that [LaBute's] talents go beyond glibly vicious storytelling and extend into thoughtful analyses of a world rotten with original sin."   —**Ben Brantley**, *New York Times*

"LaBute takes us to shadowy places we don't like to talk about, sometimes even to think about . . ."   —**Erin McClam**, *Newsday*

WRECKS

"Superb and subversive . . . A masterly attempt to shed light on the ways in which we manufacture our own darkness. It offers us the kind of illumination that Tom Stoppard has called 'what's left of God's purpose when you take away God.'"   —**John Lahr**, *The New Yorker*

"A tasty morsel of a play . . . The profound empathy that has always informed LaBute's work, even at its most stringent, is expressed more directly and urgently than ever here."   —**Elysa Gardner**, *USA Today*

"*Wrecks* is bound to be identified by its shock value. But it must also be cherished for the moment-by-moment pleasure of its masterly portraiture. There is not an extraneous syllable in LaBute's enormously moving love story."

—**Linda Winer**, *Newsday*

FAT PIG

"The most emotionally engaging and unsettling of Mr. LaBute's plays since *bash* . . . A serious step forward for a playwright who has always been most comfortable with judgmental distance."

—**Ben Brantley**, *New York Times*

"One of Neil LaBute's subtler efforts . . . Demonstrates a warmth and compassion for its characters missing in many of LaBute's previous works [and] balances black humor and social commentary in a . . . beautifully written, hilarious . . . dissection of how societal pressures affect relationships [that] is astute and up-to-the-minute relevant."   —**Frank Scheck**, *New York Post*

THE DISTANCE FROM HERE

"LaBute gets inside the emptiness of American culture, the masquerade, and the evil of neglect. *The Distance From Here*, it seems to me, is a new title to be added to the short list of important contemporary plays."   —**John Lahr**, *The New Yorker*

THE MERCY SEAT

"Though set in the cold, gray light of morning in a downtown loft with inescapable views of the vacuum left by the twin towers, *The Mercy Seat* really occurs in one of those feverish nights of the soul in which men and women lock in vicious sexual combat, as in Strindberg's *Dance of Death* and Edward Albee's *Who's Afraid of Virginia Woolf.*"   —**Ben Brantley**, *New York Times*

"A powerful drama . . . LaBute shows a true master's hand in gliding us amid the shoals and reefs of a mined relationship."

—**Donald Lyons**, *New York Post*

THE SHAPE OF THINGS

"LaBute . . . continues to probe the fascinating dark side of individualism . . . [His] great gift is to live in and to chronicle that murky area of not-knowing, which mankind spends much of its waking life denying."   —**John Lahr**, *The New Yorker*

"LaBute is the first dramatist since David Mamet and Sam Shepard—since Edward Albee, actually—to mix sympathy and savagery, pathos and power."

—**Donald Lyons**, *New York Post*

"*Shape* . . . is LaBute's thesis on extreme feminine wiles, as well as a disquisition on how far an artist . . . can go in the name of art . . . Like a chiropractor of the soul, LaBute is looking for realignment, listening for a crack."

—**John Istel**, *Elle*

BASH

"The three stories in *bash* are correspondingly all, in different ways, about the power instinct, about the animalistic urge for control. In rendering these narratives, Mr. LaBute shows not only a merciless ear for contemporary speech but also a poet's sense of recurring, slyly graduated imagery . . . darkly engrossing."

—**Ben Brantley**, *New York Times*

NEIL LABUTE is an award-winning playwright, filmmaker, and screen-writer. His plays include: *bash*, *The Shape of Things*, *The Distance From Here*, *The Mercy Seat*, *Fat Pig* (Olivier Award nominated for Best Comedy), *Reasons to be Pretty* (Tony Award nominated for Best Play), *In a Forest, Dark and Deep*, a new adaptation of *Miss Julie*, *The Way We Get By*, *Reasons to be Happy,* and *Reasons to be Pretty Happy*. He is also the author of *Seconds of Pleasure*, a collection of short fiction, and a 2013 recipient of a Literature Award from the American Academy of Arts and Letters.

Neil LaBute's film and television work includes *In the Company of Men* (New York Critics' Circle Award for Best First Feature and the Filmmaker Trophy at the Sundance Film Festival), *Your Friends and Neighbors*, *Nurse Betty*, *Possession*, *The Shape of Things*, *Lakeview Terrace*, *Death at a Funeral*, *Some Velvet Morning*, *Ten x Ten*, *Dirty Week-end*, *Full Circle*, *Billy & Billie*, *Van Helsing*, and *The I-Land*.

Dracula

a thriller in 2 acts

a free adaptation by
Neil LaBute

based on the novel by
Bram Stoker

THE OVERLOOK PRESS
NEW YORK, NY

for all the children of the night

"I want you to believe . . . to believe in things you cannot . . ."
Bram Stoker

Preface

You always remember your first.

That's true enough in many things—from pizza to movies to love itself—but probably never more so than your first encounter with the Prince of Darkness.

Dracula.

Most people, no matter what their age or station in life, can recall with some clarity when they first read about, saw or heard tell of the Count—comic book, movie, radio play or the source novel itself. You hear the tale of the human bat and your life is never the same again. You begin to fear the dark, you start to turn lights on in the house where you never did before and you shudder as you walk past old churches and cemeteries in your neighborhood or city. Or any city, for that matter.

The character of Count Dracula is one that has almost mystical powers—an ability to haunt your mind and torment your dreams like no literary figure before or since.

Bram Stoker, by all accounts an Irishman as well known for being the personal secretary to the actor Henry Irving as for being an author, dashed off a nightmarish story in the late 1800s told through letters, news accounts and journal entries (which sounds decidedly undramatic) and changed literature—or at least one kind of literature—virtually overnight. His epistolary horror novel was an instant success and cause célèbre, and while he never again wrote anything as widely and wildly read as his fictional monster, he was single-handedly responsible for making the night and bats and vampires something to fear and loathe and dread.

I remember vividly the Saturday afternoon of my youth when Bela

Lugosi first appeared on our black-and-white television screen and tore into the necks of his victims and into my poor young psyche in equal measure—it created a lifelong love of, respect for and fascination with the creature that hasn't waned to this day. Some of earliest vampire memories come from watching the Gothic soap opera *Dark Shadows* with my mother, who (God bless her soul) would allow me to stay home from school at least once each week until the show was finished and then take me into the office with a handwritten note with various excuses, from "sore throat" to "car troubles." That good woman instilled an appreciation of literature, film and little white lies that I still deal with today. Mom loved to be scared—as if life with my father wasn't scary enough—and so we watched Dracula and all sorts of other monsters and killers in various forms during my youth; me appreciating both the mood and mechanics of how fear operated on the viewer and my mother just appreciating a good old-fashioned jump scare.

Years later, I was asked to adapt the great novel to the stage for a Shakespeare festival that operated in Utah (playing in a magnificent outdoor stone amphitheater that was originally built during the Depression as a WPA project on the grounds of the state psychiatric hospital in Provo). It was a difficult and challenging task but I thoroughly enjoyed one of my earliest tastes of moving a story from one medium to another and it was also here that I had my first real encounter with the character of Abraham Van Helsing, whom I decided to change into a female character (as my work on the project was taking a strongly feminist turn the more I adapted the piece to the stage). I will let you, dear reader, explore that further as you read my adaptation of the novel but know this: my respect and appreciation of the source material is strong and, hopefully, extremely evident on each and every page.

Years later, I found myself returning to a female version of the Van Helsing character when I was approached by two friends in the television industry, Chad Oakes and Mike Frislev, of Nomadic Pictures. We had worked together on a wonderful Western of theirs, *Hell On Wheels*, and they spoke to me about creating and running a show called *Van Helsing,* based on elements of Stoker's book but with a rather modern take on it: a post-apocalyptic tale of one of Abraham's descendants who just might be the savior of humanity after the earth is overrun by vampires (thanks to such clever plotting as a super volcano exploding in Yellowstone that allows for darkness to cover the land both day and night). It's good, old-fashioned, blood-soaked genre fun and I enjoyed my work on the show immensely. We were (and still are) blessed with an amazing cast and a group of writers who are absolute geeks and wonderful wordsmiths, and together we have had a blast envisioning a world of good and evil that will ultimately lead to some member of the Van Helsing clan coming to a reckoning with "The Dark One" (we never say the name "Dracula" in our version of the story, but you know who we mean).

And all because some fellow named Bram Stoker had a fever dream that he turned into one of the best-selling and mind-blowing stories of any generation.

Pretty impressive stuff.

So many great (and horrible) films and comic books and operas and Broadway musicals and so on and so on have risen from this source material—for every great one (like both versions of *Nosferatu* and Carl Theodor Dreyer's *Vampyr* and Tod Browning's seminal *Dracula*) there are probably ten bad ones, but I faithfully attend them all, wait for the lights to go down and pray that this one will scare the living shit out of me—and sometimes it does. Even when it doesn't, though, it takes me on a ride that is singular and meaningful and unlike any other escape that I make into the arts.

Maybe it's the darkness in my own soul that always secretly roots for the Count—I always hope that he'll escape this wooden stake or that new dawn or some broken piece of the cross that will inevitably impale him and turn him into a smoldering pile of ashes. Rarely does it happen— even in such delicious new twists on the myth by auteurs like Claire Denis, Tony Scott, Ana Lily Amirpour, or Jim Jarmusch.

But the undead are resilient creatures and hard to kill—they rise again and chase us through our dreams and into the night. That's what I really love about them (and Dracula himself): they don't give up. Vampires aren't quitters, no matter how much they'd like to be. They are fated to try and try and try again and that's how I feel about writing in general—it's something I love and hate and fear and desire and I can never give it up, no matter what happens to me in this life.

I am a creature of the page and I plan to haunt theaters and cinemas and your Netflix account long after I've shuffled off this mortal coil—and you can thank or curse, in part at least, Mr. Bram Stoker for that.

May you enjoy the following version of this classic story—it was a pleasure to write (with just enough pain thrown in to make it all worthwhile).

Neil LaBute
June 2019

Act 1

A crash of thunder, a flash of lightning.

The crumbling remains of a grand ballroom at Castle Dracula is disclosed.

A great wooden table is the centerpiece of the room, with it and much of the other furniture hidden beneath yards of faded sheeting.

Another dash of lightning and a figure is revealed at the table, huddled near a single flickering candle. WILLIAM RENFIELD, *a small, proper man of about 30, scratches hastily in his journal, reading aloud as he does.*

RENFIELD "5 June. Transylvania. I have not slept well, for I have had all sorts of queer dreams. My coach here has been comfortable enough, but there have been wolves howling near the roadside night upon night, which surely has something to do with my fatigue.

Lightning and thunder burst loudly.

"This evening, I became conscious of the fact that the driver was in the act of pulling up the horses in the courtyard of a vast ruined castle, from whose towering black windows came no ray of light, and whose broken battlements showed a jagged line against the moonless sky. I must have been asleep, for certainly if I had been fully awake I would have noticed the approach of a . . ."

Another cascade of lightning and thunder. In that moment, DRACULA *appears at* RENFIELD'*s side. A Romantic figure of indistinguishable age and sex, dressed in flowing black and white. A jagged sash of red worn at the throat collar. A face hidden in darkness.*

A hand is placed on RENFIELD*'s arm, who physically starts, nearly slipping from his chair. He turns slowly to look up at* DRACULA, *pen dropping to the floor and rolling along the flagstone.*

DRACULA . . . I am Dracula, and I bid you welcome.

RENFIELD Coun . . . Count Dracula?

DRACULA For myself, I disdain the use of titles. So very old-fashioned . . . (*Smiles.*) And you are Mr. Renfield?

RENFIELD . . . yes.

DRACULA Welcome to my home. Come freely, go safely and leave something of the happiness you bring!

RENFIELD Thank you, I . . .

DRACULA Come, the night air is chill, and you must eat and rest.

DRACULA *moves quickly to the table, pulling the linen dust sheet off with a flourish. Beneath it is an elaborate banquet.*

Please forgive that no one was available to greet you upon your arrival. Let me see to your comfort myself.

DRACULA *remains standing and pours* RENFIELD *a glass of dark red wine.*

I pray you, be seated; now sup as you please. You will, I trust, excuse me that I do not join you, for I have dined already.

RENFIELD Of course, thank you . . .

RENFIELD *begins to reach for the nearest dish, but remembers first to hand over a letter to* DRACULA.

From my employer, Mr. Peter Hawkins. He sends his apologies for not being able to make the journey.

As RENFIELD *begins to eat,* DRACULA *reads the letter.*

DRACULA "I am happy to say I can send a sufficient substitute, of whom shall take your instructions in all matters." Marvelous . . .

The sudden howling of wolves pierces the darkness. DRACULA *rises and moves toward a towering window.*

   Ahhh, listen to them . . . the children of the night. What music they make!

RENFIELD *seems unmoved by this, returning to his meal.* DRACULA *watches him, almost saddened by this reaction.*

RENFIELD Bloody wolves, howled at us nearly all the way from Vienna . . .

DRACULA Ah, sir, you dwellers of the city cannot enter into the feelings of the hunter. Into the spirit of our nightly hunt . . .

RENFIELD Well, I know enough to stay out of the woods at night while they're about. Good sense tells me that . . .

DRACULA But without the night we are not whole. We are only half ourselves.

DRACULA *motions* RENFIELD *to come to the window.*

   Come, look into the dark. What is it you see?

RENFIELD Nothing. Well, I mean . . . blackness, that's all. A void. Frightening. (*Beat.*) And you, Dracula, what do you see?

DRACULA . . . the Garden of Eden.

RENFIELD *studies* DRACULA *for a moment, pulling away slightly.* RENFIELD *returns to his place at the table, trying to make conversation as he does.*

RENFIELD Yes, well . . . to each his own, I suppose. (*Beat.*) I, ahh, took the liberty of looking about when I arrived. Since I couldn't find you, you see, I wandered around a bit. It's quite a place . . .

DRACULA Yes, glorious in its day.

RENFIELD Your library is enormous . . .

DRACULA *sits suddenly in a chair near* RENFIELD, *watching the young Englishman as he eats.*

DRACULA *leans in more closely to* RENFIELD, *making him move back almost involuntarily.*

Come, tell me of the house you have procured for me . . .

RENFIELD *nods, wiping his mouth and reaching into his bag. He moves several dishes and produces a sheath of paper that he proceeds to spread out. Using his knife,* RENFIELD *points to several key locations of a faded ground plan while he speaks.*

RENFIELD Well . . . the estate is called Carfax and it contains some twenty acres, surrounded by a solid wall. The . . . the house itself is large and dates back to medieval times . . . it's quite secluded, with only a large private lunatic asylum close at hand. I do hope this doesn't dissuade you—it is not visible from Carfax itself.

DRACULA I am glad that it is old and big. I myself am of an old family, and to live in a new dwelling would kill me . . . (*Beat.*) I love the shade and the shadow, and would wish to be alone with my thoughts when I may.

DRACULA *places a friendly hand on* RENFIELD's *own.* RENFIELD *pulls away politely, starting to speak again.*

RENFIELD Yes, well . . . this would be ideal, then. Now, on the western border of the property . . . OWWW!

RENFIELD *has caught himself with the knife point, drawing blood.* DRACULA's *eyes lock on* RENFIELD's *finger as the young man holds it up and examines it.*

DRACULA Take care . . .

He reaches for RENFIELD's *hand, slowly pulling it to his open mouth. He places* RENFIELD's *finger in his mouth and slowly sucks on it.*

RENFIELD . . . take care how you cut yourself. In my country, it is more dangerous than you think.

RENFIELD *slowly pulls his finger from* DRACULA*'s mouth and wraps a handkerchief around his hand.*

Quite alright, only a scratch . . . now, shall we?

DRACULA No, no . . . after a journey such as yours, you must rest. (*Beat.*) Some rooms have been prepared . . . you may go anywhere you wish, except where the doors are locked, where of course you will not want to go . . .

RENFIELD And why do you . . .?

DRACULA There is a reason why all things are the way they are . . . we are in Transylvania, and Transylvania is not England.

RENFIELD I quite agree, my dear Count, but—

DRACULA Our ways are not your ways, and there shall be to you many strange things . . . I trust you will forgive me, but I have much work to do in private this evening.

RENFIELD *hurries and stands with bags in hand, meaning to follow.* DRACULA *raises a finger, stopping him in his tracks with an ominous warning.*

Let me advise you, dear friend . . . nay, let me warn you with all due seriousness, that you should not leave your room tonight. Be warned!

Flash of lightning, crash of thunder. RENFIELD *wheels about, wide-eyed. When he looks back,* DRACULA *has vanished. Gone.* RENFIELD *is left alone in the dark room.*

RENFIELD . . . hello? Count Dracula . . .? (*Beat.*) Oh my . . .

The sound of wolves again fills the night.

Music up as scene shifts to:

A sumptuous library— MINA MURRAY, *a beautiful, raven-haired girl of 23, sits on a lounge, finishing a letter. She reads aloud as she writes.*

MINA "9 July. My dearest Lucy, forgive my long delay in writing, but I have simply been overwhelmed as of late. The life of an assistant schoolmistress is sometimes trying, and what with the arrangements for our wedding . . . again, please forgive me. I look forward to your return here to Richmond, as I am unnerved by the asylum itself but long for the time when we can talk together freely and again build our castles in the air."

MINA *is unaware that* JONATHAN HARKER, *a handsome young man of 25, has entered the library and is quietly moving to her. He sits beside her and buries his head in her neck. She reacts, pulling away.*

MINA Jonathan!

JONATHAN I thought I might find you here.

MINA Just dashing off a letter to dear Lucy . . .

JONATHAN My sweet darling Mina—head so full of ideas and words. You never stop, do you?

MINA What do you mean by that, Jonathan? I'm only . . .

JONATHAN Nothing harmful, I assure you . . . just that you're always . . . well, you know . . . *thinking.*

MINA *studies him for a moment.*

MINA And is that so horrible?

JONATHAN No, no, not at all . . . in its place. We've just so much to do, what with the wedding, and moving to our new home . . . not much time for all this idle . . . well, you know what I mean.

MINA No, Jonathan, I don't . . .

JONATHAN I'm just not sure that another note to Lucy is so very vital . . . you'll see her in a matter of weeks as it is.

MINA . . . yes, but . . .

JONATHAN I could use some help . . . I mean, putting things into place before Transylvania. (*Beat.*) You might jump in and lend a hand, you know. You are going to be my wife, after all . . .

MINA I don't really see where that's of any consequence . . .
(*Smiles.*) I mean, in terms of the matter at hand.

JONATHAN All I'm saying, dearest, is that priorities are the key.
We must know our role and keep to it . . . (*Beat.*) I'm sure if you
thought about it, you'd feel the same.

JONATHAN *tries to place a comforting arm around* MINA *but she shakes
it off.*

MINA Are you looking for a wife, John . . . or a *trained monkey*?

JONATHAN This is silly . . . let's stop.

MINA No, let's not . . . are we to have *rules* in our marriage, then?
I thought we built our feelings for one another around sharing,
around mutual respect for each another . . .

JONATHAN Good God, I hadn't counted on this, Mina . . . are we
going to argue on my last day here?

MINA If we must.

There is an uncomfortable silence. JONATHAN *squirms for a moment,
unsure of how to deal with this mini-revolution.*

JONATHAN Oh, Mina . . .

MINA I'm sorry Jonathan . . . I'm, I don't know, I just want more than
is merely *expected* of me. Expected of my being a woman . . .

JONATHAN I'm not trying to *suppress* you, Mina . . . look, we've
fought this battle a dozen times . . . I love you for what you are.
The entire you. Your complexities, your, your . . . simplicities . . .
you. (*Beat.*) I just believe that certain things should be . . . like
certain things.

MINA Such as?

JONATHAN Such as . . . well, you are a female! You are going to be
my wife.

MINA And?

JONATHAN Mina . . . just *things*. I mean, do expect me to carry our children? Nurse them? Hmmm?

MINA I wish you could.

JONATHAN We each have our *place*, Mina . . . it's the laws of nature, my dear. Human nature.

MINA Then perhaps nature is wrong . . . perhaps I need something other than what this world always prescribes for us . . . it's women.

JONATHAN, *exasperated, turns away.*

JONATHAN Perhaps you want something other than *me*!

At this MINA *stops and looks at* JONATHAN. *A smile slowly crosses her lips.*

MINA I've done it again, haven't I?

JONATHAN Yes . . . a bit.

MINA I'm sorry, I just can't . . .

JONATHAN I do so want you to be happy, Mina.

She smiles and puts her head on his shoulders.

MINA Then have no fear, my love . . . for you make me as happy as anyone can be. Truly . . .

They kiss lightly.

JONATHAN As soon as I return I'm going to take you away. We'll be married next month. We won't wait until Christmas. We'll stretch out our honeymoon month to three and be in the house by autumn.

MINA Oh John, do you think we could?

JONATHAN Of course, why not? Mother wanted us to wait, but she'll understand. And I want to get you away . . .

He moves to her, kissing her again. She responds, but pulls away after a moment.

Why do you shrink away when I kiss you? Sometimes you're mysterious, Mina. So distant . . .

She leans back against him, pulling his arms up around her for warmth and protection.

MINA Forgive me, dear. I am yours, all yours. (*Beat.*) I've just so much in my head these days . . . your journey to the continent, which troubles me, and . . .

JONATHAN Think nothing of that, Mina . . . I'll be back in a fortnight, or a little more.

MINA Still, it's such a terribly long . . .

JONATHAN Yes, but Mr. Hawkins has been insistent . . . and besides, poor Renfield. A good man, to be sure, and took this trip as a favor to me. Now he's disappeared! Can't very well run off and leave my own colleague in such a God-forsaken place . . .

MINA *shudders a bit, burying herself deeper into* JONATHAN's *arms.*

 . . . don't be frightened.

MINA I can't help myself, Jonathan. I feel the world watching us . . . like a thousand fiery eyes in the dark. A world we've no control over.

JONATHAN I'll protect you, my pet. I've pledged myself to the task . . .

She wraps his arms around herself more tightly.

MINA If only you can, Jonathan . . . if only you can.

Music up as scene shifts to:

*Castle Dracula—*RENFIELD, *with a candle at his elbow, is writing in his journal at a small desk.*

RENFIELD "10 July. All seems lost today . . . have been a virtual prisoner at Castle Dracula these four weeks past, and can see no end in sight. I quite doubt that any dreams can be more terrible than the most unnatural, horrible net which seems to be closing around me. My only hope now lies with Mr. Hawkins and my friend and associate, Jonathan Harker. May God send them to deliver me!"

RENFIELD *finishes this passage and closes his journal. He yawns widely and, picking up the candle, moves to his bed. As he nears the bed and candlelight, a* BEAUTIFUL YOUNG WOMAN *in white lying on his bed is revealed. He gasps and steps back. She smiles at him. He begins to pull away and she kisses him, moving directly into the open arms of* ANOTHER WOMAN *in white. Suddenly, they begin to pull him to the floor.* RENFIELD *tries to protest vocally but his mouth is covered. Finally, with a last effort, he breaks away, dashing wildly about the room, the women advancing on him all the time. As they close in on him, he backs toward a window.*

Stay away . . . I warn you, I'll . . . I'll jump! I . . .

RENFIELD *backs up another step and is enveloped in the dark, outstretched arms and cape of* DRACULA.

DRACULA *quickly covers him and* RENFIELD *disappears. The women stop, hissing at* DRACULA, *who controls them with a warning.*

DRACULA How dare you touch him, either of you? You dare to cast eyes on him, enter his room, when I have already forbidden it? Back, I tell you! This man is mine, belongs to me! Beware that you forsake my love . . .

One of the women laughs, moving bravely toward DRACULA.

WOMAN 1 "Love?!" You know *nothing* of love!

The other woman steps forward.

WOMAN 2 You've never loved!!

They laugh in unison until DRACULA's *hands, in a flash, curl around the neck of the nearest woman. He pulls her close as* RENFIELD *tumbles to the floor, unconscious.*

DRACULA Yes, I too can love; you both can remember it from the past. Is it not so? Well, now I promise you that when I am done with him you shall kiss him and have him as you wish. Now go! GO!! I must awaken him.

DRACULA *releases the woman, but they seem reluctant to leave.*

Back, back I tell you, to your own place! Your time is not yet come . . . Wait! Have patience! Tonight is mine, tomorrow will be yours!!

WOMAN 1 Are we to have *nothing* tonight?

WOMAN 2 Feed us.

DRACULA *looks at them and nods silently. He points to a bag near the window, which the women jump toward and tear open. The muffled wail of a half-smothered child can be heard. Laughing, the women scoop up the bag and disappear into the dark.* DRACULA *kneels slowly and picks* RENFIELD *up.*

DRACULA Awake, my friend, for there is much work to be done . . .

RENFIELD*'s eyes flutter open as* DRACULA *sinks teeth deep into the young man's neck.*

Crash of thunder and lightning.

Music up as scene shifts to:

*A sumptuous library—*MINA *sits at a desk, reading aloud to* LUCY WESTENRA, *a stunning beauty of 25.* LUCY *is golden-haired, dressed in flowing white, and listening intently to her friend as she skims a letter.*

MINA "23 July. Buda-Pesth. Dearest Mina, I am sad to report that I have not located Renfield nor this person known as Dracula. The local towns people will speak of said Count only in whispers and widened eyes. Moreover, the sprawling Castle Dracula stands deserted and in ruins, and I can find no sign of it having been inhabited in years . . . I will continue my search, but am afraid that

I must return soon. Am constantly tired, as my sleep has been per-
sistently interrupted by the most disturbing of dreams . . ."

MINA *stops for a moment, then folds the letter up and replaces it in its
envelope.*

The rest is much the same, I'm afraid . . .

LUCY Yes. But I'm sure Jonathan's quite alright, though . . .

MINA Oh, I don't fear that, not so much, anyway . . . he's very gentle
in the closing passages, pledging himself to me. (*Beat.*) I'm just
worried that his return will be hampered in some way. You know,
strange land and all that.

LUCY I shouldn't worry about it . . . he's a good, strong man.

MINA My dear Lucy, I think being a man has little to do with it.

LUCY *smiles at this.*

LUCY Ah! Still reading your *pamphlets*, I see . . .

MINA *blushes, turning away.*

MINA And if I am? There's nothing wrong with a bit of self-awareness,
Lucy.

LUCY Only at the cost of offending our fiances . . . (*Beat.*) Remember,
we're both to be married within the year.

MINA Yes, and I'm determined to be a most excellent wife.

LUCY I'm so happy to hear . . .

MINA But I will not be seen as anyone's weaker vessel. I will *not*.
(*Beat.*) Don't you agree?

LUCY I'm not so sure . . . at school I would have jumped to
your side. But now, about to marry Arthur and as happy as I am
. . . I think better a shallow vessel than an unused bowl on the
shelf. No?

In spite of herself, MINA *joins* LUCY *in a good laugh.*

MINA Oh, Lucy, I can't tell you how marvelous it is to have you home! And Arthur, well, he's a different man now that you're around . . .

LUCY He is wonderful, isn't he?

MINA Yes. And quite devoted to his work here . . .

LUCY Such a man of science.

MINA Yes.

LUCY And Jonathan . . .

MINA Oh yes . . .

They sit for a moment in silence, each thinking about the man in their respective lives.

MINA We're awfully lucky, aren't we?

LUCY Quite. (*Beat.*) And not a dark cloud on the horizon to spoil it for us.

MINA . . . no. Quite right.

MINA *moves to the window seat where* LUCY *is sitting. Like schoolgirls, they huddle together as they begin to talk.*

Now I won't wait a moment longer. In your letters you promised to tell me everything about the engagement . . . I've hounded Arthur about it, but you know how men can be. The bravest of the lot becomes a stammering mess when discussing the altar!

LUCY *smiles at this. Nods in agreement.*

LUCY Oh Mina, how can I tell you? These last few weeks have been the *most* marvelous of my life. This past spring, Arthur and I met and fell in love . . . he's so handsome, isn't he?

MINA Yes, he is. And from the looks of it, quite well off . . .

LUCY Well, he is of good birth. Just think, only nine and twenty and yet has this enormous lunatic asylum under his own care . . .

At that moment, DR. ARTHUR SEWARD, *a purposeful, somewhat dashing man of almost 30, pokes his head into the room.*

ARTHUR   Anyone fancy lunch on the lawn . . . say, in half an hour
   or so?

LUCY *is immediately on her feet, running to him and throwing her arms around his neck. She playfully bites his neck.*

   Goodness, Lucy, do show a bit of restraint . . . we have guests.

MINA   Oh, don't mind me, Arthur . . . I'm very forgiving in the face
   of passion.

ARTHUR   Yes, well, I'm afraid young Lucy here is rather open with
   her, umm, *emotions* . . . something she's forever trying to change
   about me.

LUCY   Nothing wrong with showing one's love, is there?

ARTHUR   As a rule of thumb, no . . . in public, however, my dearest
   angel, quite arguable.

LUCY   Hmmm . . . if the Lord Byron were here he'd say, and I quote . . .

ARTHUR *places a playful hand over* LUCY*'s mouth.*

ARTHUR   Well, he's not here, thank the Lord, or I'm afraid I'd spend
   all my time keeping an eye on the two of you! And please don't
   quote that rake in my home.

LUCY   "Our" home, don't you mean, my love?

ARTHUR   Yes, yes, I do . . . very shortly.

MINA   Won't you, umm, tell us about your engagement then, Arthur?
   I'd love to hear . . .

ARTHUR   Oh, ahhh . . . well, best left to . . . got a few things to finish
   up in the office . . . 'nother time, perhaps . . .

ARTHUR *releases* LUCY, *moving awkwardly toward the door.*

   Don't forget now, lunch at half past . . .

ARTHUR *turns back to the women as if to add something, but mumbles to himself and exits.* LUCY *and* MINA *watch him go, then laugh to themselves.*

MINA Didn't I tell you? Such a brilliant man and so absolutely tongue-tied when it comes to the two of you . . .

LUCY And I love him all the more for it! (*Beat.*) Ohh, it's a wonderful thing, isn't it, Mina?

MINA What's that?

LUCY The love of a man . . .

MINA Yes . . . yes it is. But I think it's *love* itself that's the really marvelous thing.

MINA *pulls* LUCY *over to a divan and they sit together.*

LUCY . . . have you ever been unsure of your love for Jonathan?

MINA Not since I committed to it. The principles of a woman's happiness are well established, Lucy. She is to love her home and her children without reservation, and too, she must realize that it is her total devotion to her husband that makes these things possible for her . . . (*Beat.*) Of course, it occasionally requires small deceptions to keep said men thinking that we are less capable than they . . .

LUCY All that, and yet you say you love Jonathan completely?

MINA Oh yes . . . if one is to be loved and respected, one must be steadfast in one's *own* commitments. (*Beat.*) I'm simply suggesting that one must also love with their eyes wide open . . .

LUCY Mina . . .

MINA Now, enough of my philosophies . . . are you committed to Arthur in this same way?

LUCY Without question . . . I love him and no other . . .

MINA Are you sure?

LUCY Yes I am, Mina.

MINA Then I'm very happy for you . . .

MINA *turns away, not wanting to see her in a moment of* distress.

LUCY Oh, you poor darling, here I am talking in trivial generalities! You mustn't worry . . . Jonathan will be back before you know it, and we shall both have husbands. You'll see . . .

MINA Oh Lucy, you are such a dear . . . I do hope you're right. (*Beat.*) And yet . . .

LUCY What is it, Mina?

MINA *looks out the window, clutching her letter from* JONATHAN *tightly in one hand. She shivers a bit.*

MINA I'm not sure . . . not sure at all. It's just . . . I feel something coming. Something *cold.* (*Beat.*) Perhaps it's nothing, a passing storm. Still, it's odd for this time of year . . .

LUCY It does feel a bit like rain . . .

MINA . . . so very odd.

Music up as scene shifts to:

Blast of storm effects. Lights up on five areas: MINA *and* LUCY *in the library, writing at small tables;* ARTHUR *sitting on a bench, reading from the newspaper; a* SEA CAPTION *on deck scribbling in his log;* RENFIELD, *looking deranged, hiding in the bowels of the ship talking to himself.*

Wind howls and the sails of the ship drop into view and move dramatically back and forth.

ARTHUR "8 August. Whitby. One of the greatest and most sudden storms on record has just been experienced here . . ."

LUCY "Another week gone, and no news from Jonathan. The suspense is becoming dreadful. If only Mina knew where to write or where to go to, I should feel better, but no one has heard a word since his last letter . . ."

MINA "Lucy is more excitable than usual, but otherwise well. She has taken to sleep-walking as of late, and there is an odd concentration about her which I do not understand. Even in her sleep it seems as if she is watching me . . ."

RENFIELD The Master is coming . . .

CAPTAIN "8 August. Log of the 'Demeter.' There seems some doom over this ship . . . men all gripped in a state of panic. Last night another man lost—disappeared. Feared there might be some trouble, so a search of the ship was conducted. We left no corner untouched, yet found only several large wooden crates in the hold which we are transporting to . . ."

ARTHUR ". . . then without warning, the tempest broke. The waves rose in growing fury, each overtopping its fellow, 'til in a very few minutes the foaming sea was like a roaring and devouring monster . . ."

RENFIELD The Master IS COMING!

LUCY "Woke to find myself sitting in a courtyard, overlooking the sea . . . how strange. What's happening to me? Early this morning Mina found me, and afterward I tried hard to explain myself as best I could. I felt glad that Jonathan was not on the sea, although that did not quench the fear in Mina's eyes . . ."

MINA "Lucy was very restless last night, and I, too, could not find sleep. Strangely enough, Lucy did not wake, yet got up twice and dressed herself. Fortunately, each time I awoke and got her back in bed. The third time, however, I must have drifted off. (*Beat.*) It took me no little time to find her . . . a frightful, yet serene figure, sitting alone near the cemetery and watching the sea. I am *so* afraid. Where are you, my Jonathan?"

CAPTAIN "Four days in Hell. Only self and mate left to work ship—all the others gone. Dead. We are plagued and lost. God in Heaven, you have deserted us!"

RENFIELD THE MASTER IS COMING!!

Suddenly, the sound of the storm abates and music swells up. The sail flies into the air. All lights out as new, hellish light reveals DRACULA *towering in the darkness, arms outspread.* DRACULA *seems to nearly take off in flight, vanishing into the darkness.*

Music lifts up as scene shifts to:

A sumptuous library— ARTHUR SEWARD *sits reading a note out loud while an* ATTENDANT *stands nearby.*

ARTHUR "10 August. My good friend, when I have received your letter I am already coming to you. By good fortune, I could leave Amsterdam just at once. Keep all this matter to yourself and arrange that we may see the young lady upon my arrival. Until then good-bye and Godspeed. Yours, Van Helsing."

ARTHUR *returns the letter to its envelope, sitting with his thoughts.*

ARTHUR (*To self.*) Thank God, Van Helsing . . . thank God you're coming.

ARTHUR *stands and turns to the* ATTENDANT.

Now then, what of this new patient?

ATTENDANT They've let 'im leave the room again, I hear. Blimme, sir, they bolted the door on 'im, they did, I'm quite sure of it.

ARTHUR Yet this is the second time this has happened . . . and he's been with us less than a week! Only Friday last they let him escape and he tried to break into Carfax across the way . . .

ATTENDANT Well, 'e didn't come through that door sir, I was there myself this time . . . and you know it's a drop 'a thirty feet out 'is window.

The ATTENDANT *looks at the window from where he stands.*

> I tell you, sir, nothing 'uman's getting outside that cell. Can't be done. (*Beat.*) Look for y'self . . .

ARTHUR Listen, I know my own hospital! I also know I've a patient here, and for whatever reason, he continues to elude us. Now, kindly stop arguing with me and go inform the staff of my wishes. I want this man under twenty-four watch. (*Beat.*) Have them report to me when he's located. . .

ATTENDANT Y'sir.

He walks to the door muttering to himself.

> (*To self.*) Bleedin' bat, is what 'e is! 'E's flying out through them bars . . . only way to explain it.

The ATTENDANT *exits.* ARTHUR *sits alone, turning* VAN HELSING*'s letter over and over in his hands. After a moment,* MINA *bursts into the room.*

MINA Arthur, has he arrived? I was with Lucy, but I heard a carriage and came as quickly as . . .

ARTHUR No, Mina, I'm afraid not. Remember, his letter said "perhaps" as early as the 13th . . . let's not get our hopes up.

MINA How can I not?

ARTHUR Of course, I don't mean to suggest you shouldn't, just that these things take . . . (*Beat.*) It's dark out now, he's probably stopped at some inn for the . . .

MINA Oh, it seems as if he's been gone forever . . .

ARTHUR Yes, yes, I know, my dear . . . but you mustn't worry . . . Jonathan's of good stock. He'll be fine.

MINA "Good stock." (*Beat.*) You mean he's a man?

ARTHUR No . . . It's just . . . well, yes, but . . . ahhh . . .

MINA *whirls about, indignant.*

MINA I think we can rule out *manhood* as reason enough for anything . . . it certainly didn't help that poor creature they found on the ship, did it?

ARTHUR What's that?

MINA Being a man . . .

ARTHUR *clears his throat uncomfortably.*

ARTHUR Yes, well . . . perhaps you might check on Lucy, then . . .
(*Beat.*) You say you heard a carriage . . .?

ARTHUR *turns from* MINA *and crosses to the window, looking out. The door to the library swings open and in walks* DOCTOR VAN HELSING. *A strong, commanding woman in her early 50s, she is dressed in boots and traveling clothes. She stops at* MINA, *taking her hand.*

VAN HELSING Hello, my dear . . .

She crosses purposefully to ARTHUR, *whom she hugs sturdily.*

Arthur!

ARTHUR Dr. Van Helsing! I didn't expect you until . . .

They hug again, then pull away to take each other in.

. . . you look marvelous.

VAN HELSING As do you, my boy . . . a bit tired perhaps.

ARTHUR Yes, well, that's . . . sorry I wasn't downstairs to meet you, I didn't hear the . . .

VAN HELSING No need for ceremony among friends, Arthur . . . besides, if I had waited for every man who promised to meet me somewhere . . . I'd still be in my pigtails, standing in a schoolyard back in Amsterdam!

ARTHUR *blushes at this while* MINA *laughs out loud.* VAN HELSING *turns to her.*

And who is this lovely young creature? Is this your . . .?

ARTHUR Ahhh, no, afraid not, no . . . this is, umm . . .

MINA Miss Mina Murray.

MINA *strides over to* VAN HELSING *and firmly shakes hands.*

. . . I'm very pleased to make your acquaintance, Doctor.

ARTHUR *moves to them, speaking as he does.*

ARTHUR Mina's staying here at Whitby while her fiance is on the
continent. A Mr. Jonathan Harker, close friend of mine.

The three people stand together, sizing one another up as a MAID
opens the door.

MAID Excuse the interruption, sir, but Miss Lucy is awake now . . .
she's calling for . . .

ARTHUR Tell her I'll be up in a . . .

MAID No, sir, forgive me, but she's asking for Miss Mina . . .

MINA *smiles at* ARTHUR *and moves off toward the door.*

MINA I'll escort her downstairs after she's had her dinner . . . will
that be alright?

ARTHUR Yes, ahh . . .

VAN HELSING That's fine, my dear. We'll be waiting . . .

ARTHUR Tell her, Mina, won't you, that I, you know, that I'm . . .
ummm . . .

MINA Don't worry, Arthur. She'll be alright . . . she's of "good stock."

MINA *smiles and exits with the* MAID.

VAN HELSING Whatever did the young lady mean?

ARTHUR I believe it was a joke . . . at my expense.

VAN HELSING Ahh. *Good.*

She smiles and pats ARTHUR *on the shoulder.*

Still a bit of a stuffed shirt, Arthur?

ARTHUR No . . . well . . . I don't know . . .

VAN HELSING I keep telling you, my boy, since our first day of classes . . . less science, more humanity!

ARTHUR *nods his head, ushering* VAN HELSING *and himself to chairs near the desk.*

ARTHUR I know, I know . . . and I'm trying.

VAN HELSING Good. (*Beat.*) Now, about Miss Lucy, you must tell me everything. Start from the beginning . . .

ARTHUR Not much to report, really, nothing of fact, anyway . . . just that . . .

VAN HELSING Be careful not to place too much emphasis on *fact*, dear boy. (*Beat.*) There is also the unknowable . . .

ARTHUR But you always taught us . . .

VAN HELSING I know what I've taught . . . facts. Scientific reasoning. Logic. Yes. And now I realize just how many patients I've lost to my "pure" science and pig-headedness . . .

ARTHUR I see.

VAN HELSING I have begun to account for the unaccountable. The unbelievable. The un*think*able . . . (*Beat.*) We are only a candle's wick away from the caves of our ancestors, Arthur, for we all still fear the dark and the beasts who rule it . . .

ARTHUR Surely we're a bit more enlightened than that! I mean . . .

VAN HELSING Not really. I have spent the time since leaving the University om traveling far and wide . . . (*Beat.*) I am less a doctor now than I am a mystic, for I realize there is far too much I could never hope to understand in this world . . .

ARTHUR Doctor Van Helsing . . . this all seems a bit . . . ummm . . .

VAN HELSING My colleagues and I would split on much of what I believe is true. But I have seen men levitate in parts of India and in China . . . actually *watched* it! Little children born and survive with their tiny heads twisted round back to front . . . I've witnessed wolves walking on two legs and speaking sentences in the forests of Germany . . . and wars in which man and machine slaughtered each other . . . (*Beat.*) We continue to progress. Yes. To grow. Expand. As you say, "enlighten." But we are living in an age of monsters . . .

ARTHUR *stops for a moment, taking this all in.*

Forgive me . . . as you know . . . I can ramble on for no reason, but we are here for Miss Lucy. Now, what of her?

ARTHUR Just that . . . well, we were so happy! We planned to be married in less than a month, but now, I think I would gladly give up any hopes of happiness if we could cure her of this curious malady . . .

VAN HELSING And your letter seems to indicate that it is an affliction of the bloodstream . . .

ARTHUR Yes, I'm quite sure of it . . . yet I know of no disease that can destroy the blood so quickly.

VAN HELSING Anything else?

ARTHUR Well, her symptoms are curious . . . almost lifeless during the daylight hours, yet seeming to revive in the early evening and night. Bouts of sleepwalking, I mean, we've found her scampering all about the damned countryside at nearly midnight! And no recollection of it whatsoever . . .

VAN HELSING How very odd . . .

ARTHUR Really, it's just beyond me . . .

VAN HELSING Hmmm . . . any aversion to the light?

ARTHUR Well, hard to tell, really, what with her sleeping much of the day away. (*Beat.*) Although, I do recall, coming upstairs once before lunch—thought some cheering up might do. You know, personal touch and all . . .

VAN HELSING *smiles at this.*

> And I noticed she'd begun to hang heavy blankets over the
> windows to stop out the sun . . . (*Beat.*) And the marks, of course . . .

VAN HELSING *Marks?*

ARTHUR It's nothing, I'm sure . . . just two odd punctures at the
neck. Probably an insect of some sort, but . . .

At this moment the ATTENDANT *bursts through the door.*

ATTENDANT Begging your pardon, sir, but I've . . . oh, I am sorry.
I had no idea your mother was 'ere . . .

ARTHUR Damn it, you fool, this isn't my mother . . . it's . . . ohh,
never mind! What is it now?

ATTENDANT Well, I've got 'im back, I have. Thought I'd better have
a look at the grounds and there 'e was, halfway up the side 'a
Carfax again. 'Ad to be twelve feet in the air, scaling that wall, and
it just as smooth as a baby's . . .

ARTHUR Yes, yes . . . and you say you've got him secured?

ATTENDANT That I 'ave . . . but for 'ow long, who knows?

ARTHUR Fine . . . I'll be along presently. And keep an eye on him
this time!

The ATTENDANT *nods and exits.* ARTHUR *quickly gathers some books
together and begins to move toward the door.*

> (*To* VAN HELSING.) I must attend to one of my patients for a
> moment . . . but you'd probably care to rest.

VAN HELSING Nonsense! I feel most intrigued. (*Beat.*) But tell me,
what is this "Carfax" your man spoke of, I did not understand
what he was . . .?

ARTHUR Oh that. It's a monster of a house across the way—dark
for years, but recently purchased by a foreign gentleman. A Count
Dracula.

VAN HELSING "Dracula . . ."

ARTHUR You know the person?

VAN HELSING No. Should I?

ARTHUR Not at all . . . I thought perhaps . . . ummmm, you know, both from the Continent . . .

VAN HELSING How very English. (*Beat*.) Anything beyond their own fair shores is a wilderness . . . full of witches, and shadows, and people who cannot speak straight. They must all be neighbors . . .

ARTHUR I didn't mean to imply . . .

VAN HELSING Nonsense. That what you English do best . . . imply. (*Beat*) I thought I broke you of that as a student . . .

ARTHUR I am sorry, Doctor. (*Beat*.) Whatever the case, that's Carfax. Can't imagine why this fellow's so intent on breaking in there . . . wouldn't be caught dead there myself. (*Beat*.) I'll have to question him again.

VAN HELSING Perhaps you question the wrong man.

ARTHUR What do you mean?

VAN HELSING This new occupant of Carfax . . .

ARTHUR Dracula. Yes?

VAN HELSING . . . perhaps the answer lies there.

ARTHUR I can't imagine why. Quite a decent person, actually. And a charming devil, to boot . . .

VAN HELSING Come then. We shall ask the patient what secret Carfax holds . . .

ARTHUR *and* VAN HELSING *exit the room. After a moment,* MINA *enters, supporting* LUCY *around the waist. She leads her to a divan in the center of the room.*

MINA . . . and she is the most amazing woman! A doctor, from what I gather, and . . .

MINA *looks about as they both sit down.*

Hello . . . I thought they'd be waiting for us.

LUCY You can stop holding me, Mina . . . really, I feel much stronger now.

MINA I'm sorry, I just want to be sure.

LUCY It's alright, you're a dear for mothering me so. Why don't you go find Arthur and the Doctor? I'll be fine here.

MINA Lucy, are you sure?

LUCY Quite.

MINA *stands and moves toward the door. A bit cautious.*

MINA I'm sure they're just down the corridor . . . back in a moment, then.

MINA *closes the door behind her.* LUCY *lies back on the couch resting her eyes. After a moment, she rises and crosses to the French doors near the desk.*

With a flourish, she throws them open and looks out into the dark. She takes a deep breath of night air, then closes the doors behind her. As she steps away, they are blown open dramatically and framed against them is DRACULA—*who steps inside the room as the doors slowly close.* LUCY *whirls, gasping at the sight of him.* DRACULA *smiles and bows.*

DRACULA Good evening . . .

LUCY Dracula.

She turns away, blushing; she seems secretly thrilled to see DRACULA.

I didn't hear you come in . . .

DRACULA Forgive me the surprise.

LUCY It's . . . lovely to see you again. It really is good of you to come by so often. Can't thank you enough . . .

DRACULA Think nothing of it. I'm grateful to be able to visit with yourself and Miss Mina. And Mr. Seward as well. (*Beat.*) One can never have enough friends . . .

LUCY No, I suppose not . . . (*Beat.*) I myself look forward to your visits. They seem to make me feel better.

DRACULA You must not encourage me, Miss Lucy . . . or I shall make them more frequently, as I should like to.

LUCY I think we would all find that . . . I would like that very much.

She begins to step toward DRACULA, *who slowly raises a hand to her, beckoning her silently forward. Voices outside the door break the hold* DRACULA *has over the young woman—she begins to faint.*

As the door swings open and MINA *steps inside with the* MAID, DRACULA *swoops down on* LUCY *and carries her to a nearby sofa.* DRACULA *then crosses directly to* MINA *and kisses her hand lingeringly.*

DRACULA Dearest Mina . . . good evening.

MINA My dear Dracula . . . when did you . . .?

DRACULA I just dropped by. (*Beat.*) I was having a most delightful chat with Miss Lucy, but I think she is not yet strong. She began to swoon and I brought her here to rest . . .

MINA I'm sorry, I only left her for a moment . . .

DRACULA Quite alright.

MINA *quickly crosses to* LUCY, *checking her as she sleeps. She pulls a blanket from the sofa arm and places it around her.*

MINA She's sleeping now. (*Beat.*) Come, let's sit till she wakes . . . I'd love to hear more of your thoughts on literature and the like.

MINA *turns to the* MAID *and points to the door.*

(*To* MAID.) Please go find Arthur and Doctor Van Helsing . . . tell them Lucy's fainted again and to come as quickly as possible.

MAID Yes, m'um.

The MAID *exits as* DRACULA *escorts* MINA *toward two chairs near the desk. They sit together and begin to chat.*

MINA Now . . .

DRACULA *holds up a hand, silencing her.*

DRACULA So . . . you have another guest?

MINA Yes, a Doctor Van Helsing, from Amsterdam.

DRACULA (*To himself.*) So, the good doctor has arrived . . .

MINA Yes. Arthur's doing everything he can to bring Lucy's health back around. Poor, poor Lucy . . .

DRACULA And what of your Mr. Harker. I thought I might find him here tonight as well.

MINA *turns away for a moment, collecting herself.*

MINA Somewhere between Whitby and Dover, I'm afraid . . .

DRACULA He shall return tomorrow, have no fear.

MINA Really? But how can you . . .?

DRACULA A superstitious whim . . . but I have a feeling about such things. And I am often correct . . .

MINA *stares at* DRACULA *for a long moment.*

MINA You are the *most* curious person. I find myself . . . strangely . . .

DRACULA . . . yes . . .

DRACULA *slowly takes* MINA*'s hand; she smiles deeply at him.*

Music up while scene shifts to:

A bare cell — ARTHUR *and* VAN HELSING *sit on a rough bench,* ARTHUR *reading from a handful of papers while* VAN HELSING *listens intently.*

ARTHUR "The life value of flies. I rate the life of a fly on a numerical scale, roughly from one through ten . . ."

VAN HELSING And you say this is what he uses so much sugar for . . . the catching of these creatures?

ARTHUR I'm afraid so. (*Reading.*) ". . . each page is a single day. The totals enclosed represent the life values of all flies I snare in any one day. The total of those totals, quite logically, represent the life values of the spiders that I feed my flies to . . ."

VAN HELSING How intriguing. Yet you say . . .

ARTHUR Wait, there's a bit more here. (*Reading.*) "The larger total, of course, represent the ones I eat myself."

ARTHUR *lays the book down, sickened by this.*

VAN HELSING So . . . the man is zoophagous. (*Beat.*) Desires living things . . .

ARTHUR From what I can gather, yes.

VAN HELSING Most interesting . . .

The ATTENDANT *enters the cell, dragging a chained and strait-jacketed* RENFIELD *behind him. He pushes* RENFIELD *down in a corner and stands near the door.*

ARTHUR Now, my good man . . .

RENFIELD Oh no, I'm not *your* man . . . I'm no one's man, except my Master's.

VAN HELSING What does he mean by . . .?

ARTHUR *shakes his head, unsure of what to say.*

ARTHUR No idea . . . keeps babbling like this, night and day. If it's not the flies, it's the rubbish . . .

RENFIELD The Master is coming . . .

ARTHUR Look here, young fellow . . . you can't be running all over the countryside every night. That's not how it's done. (*Beat.*) Now, if this happens again you will get no more sugar to put out for your flies.

RENFIELD What do I care for flies . . . now? Flies. Flies are poor, simple things . . . lowest form of life there is. Not even worth noticing. Really, I don't care a fig for flies . . .

ARTHUR Fine, then perhaps it's your spiders we need to take . . .

RENFIELD *instantly becomes a blubbering mess, crawling on his knees to* ARTHUR *and burying his head against his leg. Crying.*

RENFIELD Oh, no, no! Not my spiders! Please leave me my spiders, they're all I have!!! Please, please, please!!!

VAN HELSING Fascinating . . .

ARTHUR Here now . . . umm, that's not quite . . . look . . . alright! You'll have your spiders!

RENFIELD *immediately stops, scurrying away and looking back at the two doctors, somewhat bored.*

RENFIELD Thanks so much . . . awfully good of you, old chap.

ARTHUR *looks at him, incredulous—*RENFIELD*'s a different man.*

ARTHUR But no more escapes . . . you must promise me.

RENFIELD Not very sporting, are we? (*Beat.*) Fine, then, promise is made . . .

ARTHUR Very well . . .

ARTHUR *stands, as does* VAN HELSING*.*

. . . now, we must get back and attend to poor Lucy. I only hope that . . .

VAN HELSING Yes, I must see her immediately.

The DOCTORS *move toward the door but* RENFIELD *suddenly springs up, pinning* ARTHUR *to the wall. The* ATTENDANT *tries to pull him off but* RENFIELD *holds his ground.*

RENFIELD I want you to send me away, now, *tonight*, in this strait-jacket! Keep me chained so I've no chance of escape. This is a sanatorium, Doctor, not a lunatic asylum. This is no place for me! My cries will disturb Miss Lucy . . . they'll give her bad dreams, Doctor Seward, bad, bad dreams!!

The ATTENDANT *finally pulls* RENFIELD, *screaming, to the ground.* ARTHUR *and* VAN HELSING *exit, but* VAN HELSING *looks back in the cell.*

VAN HELSING   Tell me young man, why are you so anxious to leave this place?

RENFIELD *only laughs. He begins to howl with laughter.*

. . . and why are you so drawn to Carfax Abbey?

RENFIELD *stops immediately, turning his wild eyes to* VAN HELSING. ARTHUR *looks back inside the room.*

RENFIELD   The Master is coming . . . my Master is coming!!

RENFIELD *begins to laugh again, a hideous, violent sound.*

Music up as scene shifts to:

*A sumptuous library—*JONATHAN *sits in a chair, thumbing through the newspaper. He reads aloud from a clipping.*

JONATHAN   "15 August. Westminster Gazette. 'The Woman in White.' During the past two or three days several children straying from or playing on the Heath have disappeared . . . when found, each stated that a mysterious woman had asked them on a walk or lured them away with candles and the like. The children, all whom have been missed at night, have been slightly torn or wounded in the throat . . ."

JONATHAN *puts the paper down in disgust.*

Good Lord! If England isn't safe, where on earth is . . .?

The door swings open and in strides VAN HELSING. *She looks about, noticing* JONATHAN *and crosses to him.*

VAN HELSING Ahhh . . . Mr. Jonathan Harker, I presume.

JONATHAN Yes. Madame Van Helsing . . .

VAN HELSING A pleasure to meet you. Your fiancée is a most lovely woman . . .

JONATHAN Thank you.

VAN HELSING Everyone will be so pleased that you've returned . . .

JONATHAN Yes, I slipped in last night, late, but I'm afraid I've wasted most of the morning in bed.

VAN HELSING No matter, you're here now.

They sit together—neither sure where to begin.

JONATHAN So, Madame . . . tell me about your husband. I've heard such a great deal about his work, and I'm fascinated by the . . .

VAN HELSING I'm not married.

JONATHAN *stops cold. Stares.*

JONATHAN But surely you . . . *you're* Doctor Van Helsing?

VAN HELSING The same. (*Beat.*) If not, I've been foolishly paying his debts all these years . . .

She laughs, patting JONATHAN *on the back.*

JONATHAN I'm sorry . . . I just . . . forgive me . . .

VAN HELSING I'm quite beyond it. (*Beat.*) It is the fate of a woman in these times, Mr. Harker . . . men are always staring at us with their mouths hanging open for one reason or another. Beauty or brains, it makes no difference . . .

JONATHAN, *unsure of what to say, wisely says nothing. After a moment, he begins to speak but is interrupted by* MINA *bursting through the door.*

MINA Jonathan! You're back!! The maid said she saw you . . .

JONATHAN Yes, my love . . .

They embrace and kiss.

Oh, how I've longed for you . . .

MINA I'm so glad you're safe, John . . .

They hug again, this time MINA *notices* VAN HELSING.

Madame Van Helsing . . . hello! I want you to meet . . .

JONATHAN Umm, we've met, actually.

VAN HELSING Yes . . . he mistook me for my husband.

MINA But you're not . . .

MINA *understands and smiles at* JONATHAN.

Oh. Quite a shock, eh, Jonathan? A marvelous, lovely shock to
us all!

JONATHAN Quite.

ARTHUR *enters the room, looking tired and troubled. He sees* JONATHAN
and visibly brightens.

ARTHUR John!

JONATHAN Arthur, good to see you, man!

*They too embrace—realizing the women are at hand, they pull quickly
away and shake hands.*

. . . you look, ahh, well, Doctor.

ARTHUR Thank you. As do you.

The women smile at one another, MINA *stepping up to* JONATHAN.

MINA Come Jonathan, you must tell me everything about your trip . . .

JONATHAN Not much to tell, actually . . . never could locate my
associate. It's as if he disappeared off the face of God's earth.

ARTHUR Wasn't he traveling to meet Castle Dracula?

JONATHAN Yes, he had to show this Dracula some estates here in
England . . . (*Beat.*) I went to the residence, or what's left of it in
Transylvania, but it's a shambles . . . I wrote to you about that.

MINA I have the letter . . .

JONATHAN Can't believe anyone's lived in the place for centuries . . . though it's the address that was wired us.

ARTHUR But Dracula's here . . . here across the way at Carfax.

JONATHAN Really?

VAN HELSING Perhaps Dracula knows something of your missing friend.

JONATHAN Possible. (*Beat.*) Then again, we did send notice that Carfax Abbey was available. Our agent only went out there to put the deal on paper. The letters may have overlapped . . .

VAN HELSING Perhaps.

JONATHAN Well, I'll approach Dracula on it when we meet.

JONATHAN *turns to* MINA, *holds out his hands.*

Come, my love, let's find a quiet corner and . . .

JONATHAN *stops short. Looks over at* ARTHUR.

Ahh, I'm a fool, forgive me, Arthur . . . your coachman told me about Lucy. Is she well?

ARTHUR She's holding on . . . (*Beat.*) In fact, that's why I'm meeting now with Doctor Van . . .

MINA Then we won't stop you with idle chat . . . come, John, let's get a meal in you and we'll go up and sit by Lucy ourselves. It'll brighten her spirits to see you home . . .

JONATHAN Whatever you like, my dearest . . .

JONATHAN *takes* MINA *by the arm and leads her toward the door. She steals a kiss from his cheek.*

VAN HELSING Careful, Mr. Harker . . . your mouth is hanging open.

JONATHAN *smiles at* VAN HELSING *and exits with* MINA. VAN HELSING *turns to* ARTHUR.

Sit, Arthur, we must talk . . .

ARTHUR Have you found out any . . .?

VAN HELSING *Sit.* Now . . . I have listened intently to you these past few days, little details that you've recalled for me, put into your journals. And each disturbs me more than the last . . . day by day Miss Lucy grows weaker, seeming to waste away . . .

ARTHUR *turns away, perhaps not strong enough to hear this.*

Ahh, perhaps there is more humanity than science in you after all, my dear boy . . . but listen to me. You must be strong! If we are to win back your Lucy, we must all be strong . . . (*Beat.*) You've analyzed her blood?

ARTHUR Yes, but there were no anemic symptoms . . . her blood was normal.

VAN HELSING Hmmm. And the transfusion yesterday morning . . . any results there?

ARTHUR She rallied during the day, color even returned to her cheeks . . . well, you saw her. Seemed fine . . .

VAN HELSING Yes. But . . .?

ARTHUR But . . . this morning she was pale and completely weak again. Complaining of bad dreams . . .

VAN HELSING Anything else?

ARTHUR Those damned marks on her throat. Two little white dots with red centers . . .

VAN HELSING This is what frightens me. (*Beat.*) I spent much of today observing your new patient . . . testing certain drugs on him. Herbs I carry. And did you know he doesn't like the smell of wolfsbane?

ARTHUR "Wolfsbane?" What's that?

VAN HELSING A plant that grows only in the wild of Central Russia . . .

ARTHUR And why did you bring it with you?

VAN HELSING As a form of preventive medicine . . .

ARTHUR And why spend time in the hospital, anyway? You're here to help Lucy, if you can . . .

VAN HELSING Arthur, you must trust me . . . your Lucy cannot stand the wolfsbane, either. (*Beat.*) Now . . . listen to what I say. Without interruption. You have heard of the dark legends of Europe—about the thing they call Vampires?

ARTHUR You mean creatures who suck the blood of the living?

VAN HELSING If you wish to call them *creatures.*

JONATHAN *returns to the room, moving toward a chair.*

JONATHAN Sorry, I forgot my . . .

VAN HELSING . . . I call them the undead.

JONATHAN *stops short, curious now.*

JONATHAN What's that then . . . telling ghost stories?

ARTHUR Vampires.

JONATHAN Oh yes . . . heard a great deal of that nonsense when I was abroad. Occult, you know, very big in Europe . . . mystic nonsense, if you ask me.

ARTHUR (*To* VAN HELSING.) Surely you don't . . .

VAN HELSING Believe in them? Surely I do believe . . .

ARTHUR You mean, that vampires actually exist . . . and one's attacked Lucy?

JONATHAN *laughs out loud at this. Waits to be joined.*

JONATHAN I'm sorry, but is that all you can offer . . .?

ARTHUR Jonathan, please! The Doctor is a woman of science and learning . . . and one of my dearest friends. I must hear her out . . .

VAN HELSING Thank you, Arthur. Believe me, Mr. Harker, I do not wish this to be true . . . but if it is, we must begin to protect ourselves.

JONATHAN Fine, then . . . exactly what is this vampire nonsense you go on about?

VAN HELSING A vampire, my friend, is a man or a woman who is dead. A thing that lives after its death by drinking the blood of the living. Its power lasts only from dusk till dawn . . . during the day it must rest in the earth in which it was buried. Night is when it chooses to prey upon the living . . .

The look at one another in silence for a moment. Silence.

JONATHAN You do have an extra cell, don't you, Arthur, just in case?

ARTHUR I don't know what to think . . . but I confess, Doctor, I can't follow the logic here.

VAN HELSING The vampire attacks the throat . . . leaving two small wounds, white with red centers. The same wound that Miss Lucy carries on her neck.

JONATHAN I've seen those marks myself . . . it could be the pin from her scarf.

VAN HELSING Perhaps. But if you are wrong, what then?

JONATHAN Doctor, Lucy's troubles can't be . . . Arthur, you can't think that . . .

ARTHUR I don't know what to think. (*To* VAN HELSING.) If it were true . . . could we take her away? Where this . . . thing can't hurt her?

VAN HELSING She will not want to go . . .

ARTHUR But why . . .?

VAN HELSING A creature such as this one has survived in a changing world for centuries . . . its victims succumb as much to charm as they do to force. It is the way of the world . . .

ARTHUR But if we tell her that her life depends on it?

VAN HELSING I'm afraid not . . . the victim of the vampire becomes its minion, linked to it in life and after death. (*Beat.*) And, God forbid, should it drink of the vampire's blood . . . it too shall become one itself.

JONATHAN Doctor, this is too much!

ARTHUR Lucy would become an unclean thing, a . . . demon?

VAN HELSING Yes . . . it is Miss Lucy's soul which would be lost. (*Beat.*) Now, I would not scare you like this, my dear boy, if I felt less certain. But it was your new patient, this Mr. . . . Renfield, that I . . .

JONATHAN "Renfield?!"

VAN HELSING Yes, I'm quite sure that was it . . . "Renfield."

ARTHUR He never gave us his name . . .

JONATHAN Surely not . . . William Renfield?

VAN HELSING I have no idea . . . he would only repeat "Renfield" to me, over and over, when questioned.

JONATHAN My God . . . how could he get . . . how long has he been at Whitby, Arthur?

ARTHUR Just past a week . . . found on board a deserted ship in the harbor. Raving mad down in the hold. (*Beat.*) The Captain was lashed to the wheel . . . throat torn wide open.

JONATHAN I must see this man . . . immediately! Please!

ARTHUR Alright, I'll . . . Doctor, you'll wait here until I return?

VAN HELSING Certainly. I need to verify a few things in my books . . .

ARTHUR Until later, then . . .

JONATHAN *nods briefly at* VAN HELSING, *then exits.* ARTHUR *smiles thinly and does the same.* VAN HELSING *moves to one of her cases and rummages through a number of papers, finally pulling out a battered text. She begins thumbing through it when* MINA *and* DRACULA *enter the room.*

MINA Hello, Doctor . . . I thought I'd find Jonathan here.

VAN HELSING I'm afraid he left with Dr. Seward for a moment . . . please sit and wait, they will return shortly. And this must be . . .

DRACULA *crosses to* VAN HELSING, *taking her hand and kissing it.*

DRACULA I am Dracula . . . good evening.

MINA Dracula has been good enough to take an interest in Lucy's health.

VAN HELSING Indeed?

MINA Yes, we stopped by this evening to check on her.

DRACULA She is well, I trust?

VAN HELSING Holding steady. (*Beat.*) She seems to revive at night . . .

DRACULA Yes, the night is . . . so alive. Does wonders for the soul. (*Beat.*) So, you have traveled from the land of the tulips to cure the nervous prostration of charming Miss Lucy? I wish you all the success . . .

VAN HELSING Thank you, Dracula.

DRACULA I'm sure you'll do wonders. I find a woman's touch so . . . revitalizing.

MINA You see, Doctor, a real person of progress, a forward thinker . . . someone who actually *believes* in a woman!

VAN HELSING . . . yes, Dracula seems very forward indeed . . .

DRACULA *smiles at her, knowingly.*

DRACULA I suppose one may appear so, but I am simply lonely. These are my only neighbors when I am here at Carfax and their trouble has touched me deeply . . .

MINA *slips a hand through the crook of* DRACULA*'s arm.*

MINA And we are more grateful for your sympathy than we can say.

VAN HELSING You, like myself, are a stranger to England, Dracula?

DRACULA Yes, but I love England and its great town of London . . . so many people, so much opportunity.

VAN HELSING Opportunity?

DRACULA I am a curious foreigner . . . to me, everything is an opportunity.

VAN HELSING I hope you don't regret having bought that old ruin across the way.

DRACULA Oh, Carfax Abbey is no ruin . . . the cobwebs are deep, but we are used to that in Transylvania.

VAN HELSING Still, it's a lonely place you've chosen . . . Carfax.

DRACULA It is, and when I hear the dogs howling far and near I think myself back in my Castle Dracula with its broken battlements.

VAN HELSING Yes . . . in fact, Mr. Harker says that your castle seemed uninhabitable when he arrived. Of course you were gone by then . . . as was Mr. Renfield.

DRACULA stares in silence at VAN HELSING for a moment.

DRACULA I'm sorry . . . I do not know a Mr. . . . the name again?

VAN HELSING "Renfield."

DRACULA Ahh, yes . . . the young estate broker that was to come to my home. Alas, he never arrived nor any word by wire . . . finally, I came to England of my own accord.

VAN HELSING What makes you think he was young then?

Silence. MINA *clears her throat uncomfortably.*

DRACULA Intuition . . . not like a woman's perhaps, but intuition none the less. (*Beat.*) My country is far and the trip is a difficult one. A simple guess . . . was I correct?

VAN HELSING As always.

MINA *jumps in to change the conversation. Moving to* DRACULA.

MINA Umm, shall we go find the others? Lucy would love to see you, I'm sure of it . . .

DRACULA That would be a delight. (*Beat.*) We'll meet again, Madame . . .

VAN HELSING   Yes, I'm sure of it.

MINA *casts a curious look at* VAN HELSING, *then leads* DRACULA *off. Just before they exit,* VAN HELSING *call them.*

You plan to remain in England long, Dracula?

DRACULA   As long as there continues to be—how does one say— opportunity.

DRACULA *whirls about and leads* MINA *off.* VAN HELSING *stands alone, watching them go. She shivers to herself as the French doors blow open furiously, the night wind rushing in.*

Music up as scene shifts to:

*A bare cell—*JONATHAN *sits on a rough bench, reading aloud.* ARTHUR *paces about the room.*

JONATHAN   "How much life is there in one life? How is it contained? Can one get more? Is death really death or only a change of life?"

JONATHAN *slams the book shut.*

He writes lucidly, and yet you say he acts a raving madman? I can't believe that . . .

ARTHUR   See for yourself . . .

The ATTENDANT *leads* RENFIELD *into the cell. He is wide-eyed and stares at* JONATHAN *throughout.*

RENFIELD   I don't know this man . . . I tell you, I've never seen this man before!!

He suddenly slams into JONATHAN, *knocking him to the ground. He tries to kick at* JONATHAN *until the* ATTENDANT *pulls him away.*

This is not a man I know! I don't know his face, I just don't know him!! Doesn't even look like anyone I've ever seen!! I DON'T know him!!

ARTHUR *helps* JONATHAN *to his feet, who is staring openly.*

ARTHUR Is it . . .?

JONATHAN Good God, William . . . what happened *to you?*

RENFIELD *smiles broadly. Bows.*

RENFIELD Hello, Johnny, how are you? Missed you ever so much . . .

The men stare at RENFIELD, *mouths open wide.*

> (*In* VAN HELSING *dialect.*) Careful, Mr. Harker, your mouth is hanging open . . .

RENFIELD *laughs widely. He tries again to attack* JONATHAN, *who backs toward the door with* ARTHUR.

> Shh . . . everyone be quiet. The Master is here . . . I can feel it.
> (*Calling out.*) Master . . . Master . . .

As the men start to leave, RENFIELD *calls to them.*

> Send me away, Dr. Seward . . . you must send me away from here!
> (*Beat.*) I'll wager Miss Lucy's dreams are worse, aren't they . . .?

JONATHAN I can't stand this . . . I have to leave . . .

He and ARTHUR *exit in a hurry. The* ATTENDANT *goes over to* RENFIELD, *forcing him to the ground.*

ATTENDANT Shut up, you, and si' down! Now, not a peep out'a ya, ya 'ear me?

RENFIELD Oh, I'll be good . . . I'll be good. I have to . . . the Master is near. I'll be so good . . .

Satisfied, the ATTENDANT *pulls out a newspaper and begins reading.* RENFIELD *starts to watch a fly that buzzes around his cell, his eyes following the elaborate flight patters.*

> . . . I won't even hurt a fly.

Suddenly, RENFIELD *lashes out—snaps up the fly and pops in his mouth. Swallows it. The* ATTENDANT *looks up, missing what happened.*

RENFIELD *smiles at him and begins to hum. The* ATTENDANT *goes back to his paper.*

Music up as scene shifts to:

*A sumptuous library and bare cell—*RENFIELD *sits alone, chains and wide-eyed.*

MINA *lies on the divan, resting.* JONATHAN *sits nearby, reading from the newspaper, while* ARTHUR *sits nearby. All of them dressed in mourning.*

JONATHAN "29 August. Westminster Gazette. 'Another Child Injured.'"

RENFIELD *call out into the dark.*

RENFIELD My Master is here . . .

JONATHAN "The child, a young girl, had the same tiny wound in the throat as had been noticed in other cases. She was terribly weak, and looked quite emaciated. When partially revived, the young child weakly replied that she had been lured away by 'a lady in white.' Furthermore . . ."

ARTHUR "A lady in white . . ."

ARTHUR *rubs at his eyes, then stares off into the distance.*

JONATHAN Sorry, old man, quite insensitive to read a thing like that aloud . . .

ARTHUR No, no . . . just still in a bit of a shock, I suppose. I can't believe she's gone . . . (*Beat.*) Lucy . . . Oh, Lucy . . .

JONATHAN *lends a supportive arm to his friend.*

JONATHAN At least she went peacefully, at least there's that . . .

ARTHUR Yes.

JONATHAN *glances with concern over at* MINA, *who stirs uncomfortably.*

MINA . . . John?

JONATHAN I'm here, my love . . .

MINA*'s eyes flutter open.*

MINA Jonathan?

JONATHAN *quickly crosses to her. Kneels down.*

There you are . . .

JONATHAN By your side, dearest, as I've pledged myself to be . . .

MINA Such bad dreams, John. Terribly . . . dark dreams. Red eyes. Flashing teeth (*Beat.*) I . . . I saw Lucy there, in my dreams. She looked beautiful.

JONATHAN There, there . . .

He holds he as she weeps softly on his shoulder.

MINA Oh John, what's happening to us . . .?

JONATHAN Mustn't think about things now, sweet Mina . . . save your strength. Sleep's the thing.

MINA Yes. (*Beat.*) You'll stay with me?

JONATHAN Of course.

MINA Promise?

JONATHAN I won't leave for a moment.

She smiles weakly, settling back on the couch. JONATHAN *returns to* ARTHUR.

She's delirious.

ARTHUR Said she saw Lucy . . . there in her dreams. My Lucy . . .

JONATHAN Come now, Arthur, got to be strong. The girl's still in shock, rambling on like that. (*Beat.*) She somehow feels responsible for . . . Lucy's . . .

ARTHUR That's ridiculous.

JONATHAN Yes, but you know the feminine mentality . . . heads always racing with any number of delusions. She fears not watching her closely enough, or that the transfusion she offered went wrong somehow. Can't seem to talk her out of it.

ARTHUR Lucy simply . . . wasn't strong enough for this world.

JONATHAN Well, whatever she was . . . she was too good for it.

ARTHUR Yes . . .

The men hug for a moment, overcome with their grief.

JONATHAN . . . and now Mina. She grows weaker by the day, you needn't try to hide it from me.

ARTHUR I'm doing all I can, John.

JONATHAN I believe you, and trust you with her life . . . (*Beat.*) When does your Doctor Van Helsing return?

ARTHUR Hopefully, by tomorrow's coach . . . although she wasn't sure how long her research might take. (*Beat.*) But I thought you didn't care for the good doctor's suggestions?

JONATHAN I must put my personal feelings aside . . . for the sake of Mina.

ARTHUR Yes . . . we must do everything in our power for her.

JONATHAN Just . . . don't expect me to stand by and listen to her silly tales of the walking dead. I mean, really, Arthur!

ARTHUR *hangs his head at this.*

ARTHUR I was . . . desperate, John. I listened because I was desperate.

JONATHAN And that, I understand . . . but we do agree, I mean, now that we're alone, man to man and talking sensibly . . . (*Beat.*) "VAMPIRES?!" This isn't the Middle Ages! . . .

ARTHUR No . . .

JONATHAN There is an honest explanation for everything, correct?

ARTHUR Yes. (*Beat.*) Except. Perhaps . . . the unexplainable.

RENFIELD My Master is here . . . my Master is here!

JONATHAN *begins to argue but is cut off by the sudden appearance of the* ATTENDANT.

ATTENDANT Begging it, sir, but 'e's going off again . . . all around the bleedin' room! I 'aven't got anyone else 'ere tonight, and I'm not sure I can 'andle 'im alone . . . don't want 'im goin' out the window, that's all. You mind?

ARTHUR Yes, I'm coming . . .

The ATTENDANT *nods and runs off.* ARTHUR *gathers his things and heads for the door.*

JONATHAN You need my assistance with him, Arthur? I do know him, after all . . .

ARTHUR That would be tremendous of you, but remember what Van Helsing said about . . .

JONATHAN Well, we'll lock the door behind us. I can't see where waking her and taking her up to bed is any better medicine than this . . .

ARTHUR *goes to the French doors as* JONATHAN *kisses* MINA *lightly.*

ARTHUR Fine, then. I'll just secure these, as well . . .

RENFIELD My Master is here . . . my Master has come for me!!

JONATHAN I can hear the poor sod from here. We'd better hurry!

ARTHUR Yes, before the entire place is in a panic!

ARTHUR *locks the doors tightly and he and* JONATHAN *hurry out of the room, taking heed to lock the library door behind them.*

Lights slowly fade to a lurid red as MINA *stirs in her sleep.*

MINA . . . John?

In her delirium, she reaches out at nothing. As she does, a hand appears from behind the couch, clutching at her own. DRACULA *suddenly materializes and pulls* MINA *close. Kisses her deeply—*

suddenly, DRACULA*'s shirt is open, revealing skin. A long nail rakes across the flesh and blood flows from the wound.*

DRACULA *draws* MINA *to the crimson and she drinks hungrily from it.* DRACULA *clutches her near and stares out at the audience.* RENFIELD *begins to cackle loudly.*

RENFIELD . . . my Master is here! My Master is here!!!

Music up as lights fade slowly out:

END OF ACT 1

Act 2

A crash of thunder, a flash of lightning.

A sumptuous library is disclosed. JONATHAN *sits at the desk, reading from a telegram.*

JONATHAN "30 August. London. Am awaiting answer to your courteous inquiry. Stop. Have contacted shipping company concerning original invoice of the ship 'Demeter.' Stop. Will wire with results in a few days. Stop. God be with Mr. Renfield and yourself. Stop. Story of your travels and Renfield's madness too horrible to believe. Stop. Yours, Mr. Peter Hawkins."

VAN HELSING *and* ARTHUR *enter the room, both looking weary and drained.* ARTHUR *is slowly rolling down his shirt sleeves.*

VAN HELSING It is all we can do for now . . .

JONATHAN What's that? Is Mina worse . . .?

ARTHUR Should I sit with her?

VAN HELSING It would not be a bad thing . . . she continues to be troubled in her sleep.

ARTHUR I just pray this transfusion will be of some help . . .

VAN HELSING Yes. (*Beat.*) I believe it vital that we keep an eye on her these next few nights . . . when it finally did happen, Miss Lucy went so quickly. I fear the same of Miss Mina . . .

JONATHAN It can't be . . . I won't allow it!

VAN HELSING Then go and stand guard near her door . . . let no one enter the room tonight.

JONATHAN Yes, I will . . .

JONATHAN *moves off and exits.* ARTHUR *watches him go, then crosses and closes the door behind him.*

ARTHUR Well, what do you think, Doctor?

VAN HELSING The symptoms are clear . . .

ARTHUR Perfectly. The same as poor Lucy's, I'm afraid. (*Beat.*) Yet, no small wounds that I could see . . .

VAN HELSING Then you did check beneath the ribbon she wears around her neck . . .

ARTHUR You mean . . .?

VAN HELSING She has it on constantly now . . . Did you think it just came into fashion?

ARTHUR No, but I . . .

VAN HELSING *smiles, shaking her head at him.*

VAN HELSING Arthur, for all your learning, you possess one of man's great gifts.

ARTHUR What's that?

VAN HELSING The amazing ability to overlook the obvious . . .

ARTHUR Yes, well, I saw the ribbon, but . . . you know . . .

The lone howl of a wolf can be heard in the distance.

There it is again! I'd swear my life that's the sound of a wolf . . .

VAN HELSING In England?

ARTHUR Strange, I know, but . . . I've heard it every night since Mina's taken ill.

VAN HELSING *goes to the French doors, looking out into the night.*

VAN HELSING I hardly think you'll find wolves prowling about Richmond, Arthur.

ARTHUR Yes, I know . . . ten miles from London . . .

VAN HELSING Still, it could be a wilderness out there . . . nothing
about as far as one can see.

ARTHUR True. Except Carfax . . .

VAN HELSING Yes, Carfax Abbey, and its very mysterious occupant.
(*Beat.*) Your friend, Dracula, came by again last night.

VAN HELSING *closes the French doors behind her.*

ARTHUR I wouldn't say Dracula's my friend, exactly . . .

VAN HELSING Dracula seems genuinely interested in Miss Mina's
case. If I did not take know better, I fear that . . .

ARTHUR What? No, Dracula's whole attitude shows it isn't that . . .
(*Beat.*) Look at the flowers sent to the funeral. The drop-by visits.
I think this is simply a person who's quite lonely.

VAN HELSING Perhaps.

Laughter is heard behind the French doors. VAN HELSING *turns to look
while* ARTHUR *dashes to the doors, pulling them open.* RENFIELD *stands
in the shadows, looking at the two doctors.*

RENFIELD Good evening, Doctors . . . I'm so glad you could pop
over for tea.

VAN HELSING Mr. Renfield . . . did you hear us talking?

ARTHUR *goes to the balcony, looking down.*

ARTHUR It's a drop of thirty feet or so . . . how could he . . .?

RENFIELD I flew . . . I flew . . . I FLEW!

ARTHUR Come now, Renfield, how did you get here?

RENFIELD Wouldn't you just love to know? But it's a secret . . .
(*Beat.*) And I have promised not to tell.

VAN HELSING Promised who?

RENFIELD *looks at* VAN HELSING, *smiling and laughing a bit.*

RENFIELD Very good, Doctor . . . very, very good.

Suddenly, the ATTENDANT *bursts in and spots* RENFIELD.

ARTHUR You!

RENFIELD *scampers behind* ARTHUR, *peering out at the* ATTENDANT.

RENFIELD Don't touch me! (*To* ARTHUR.) I don't think he really cares for me . . .

ATTENDANT And beggin' your pardon, Doctor, I know yer upset, but I 'aven't been at fault. I swear, I 'aven't.

RENFIELD You can't catch me . . . you can't catch me . . .

ATTENDANT Shuddap you! (*Beat.*) So . . . I 'ears a noise, like a wolf 'owling . . . I open 'is door to check 'im and who do I see but 'is legs goin' through the window as though 'e's gonna climb straight down. 'E ain't human, not this one . . .

VAN HELSING Climb DOWN a wall . . .?

ATTENDANT Don't expect no one to believe it, but I seen it!

ARTHUR He was climbing FACE first? This can't . . . like a bat?

ATTENDANT Funny you'd say that—I mean, about a bat. As I ran to the window, made to grab 'is feet . . . a 'uge bat flew toward the bars, tried to 'it me in the face, it did!

RENFIELD I know where the bat came from . . .

ARTHUR Where? (*Shaking him.*) Where, man, where?!

RENFIELD Out of his belfry! . . .

RENFIELD *makes a dash across the room, the others chasing after him.*

Master, help me! Help me, they're trying to catch me like a fly!!

RENFIELD, *after several near misses, runs to the door and swings it wide open.* DRACULA *stands framed in the hallway, smiling.* RENFIELD *stops cold, staring up at the Count. He backs slowly toward the* ATTENDANT *and turns to him, coolly.*

I'd like to return to my room, now. I'm sure they're done freshening up. (*Bows.*) Good night, gentlemen . . .

RENFIELD *calmly allows the* ATTENDANT *to grab him and pull him off toward the door. He nods courteously toward* DRACULA *as he is taken out.*

DRACULA Doctors. (*Beat.*) My, what a strange little man. A friend of yours?

VAN HELSING Didn't you recognize him, then, Count?

DRACULA No . . .

ARTHUR That was Mr. Renfield . . .

DRACULA Really? The fellow supposedly sent to me in Transylvania . . . (*Beat.*) But why send a lunatic?

VAN HELSING Interesting . . . he seemed to know who you were.

DRACULA I suppose my face seems a familiar one . . . who can say where a madman's thoughts lie?

VAN HELSING Seemingly his lie at Carfax.

ARTHUR What Dr. Van Helsing means to say is . . .

VAN HELSING What I AM saying is this . . . do you have any idea why Mr. Renfield has tried twice to break into Carfax Abbey? Hmm?

DRACULA Heaven knows . . .

VAN HELSING *and* DRACULA *size each other up in silence.*

VAN HELSING . . . yes, I'm sure it does.

The MAID *enters the room, calling* ARTHUR.

MAID 'Scuse me, sir, but you asked to know if the young miss were to wake up . . . she has, just this minute.

ARTHUR Thank you . . . tell her and Jonathan we'll be up momentarily. (*Beat.*) Better yet, we'll go ourselves now.

MAID Y'sir.

ARTHUR Could you, umm . . . see to the comfort of . . . Dracula . . . while we're gone?

MAID Pleasure . . .

ARTHUR Is that alright? We should only be a few . . .

DRACULA Do what you must for the young lady, please . . . (*Beat.*)
I will wait for you here. Believe me, I have all the time in the
world . . .

DRACULA *smiles warmly at the* MAID *as* ARTHUR *and* VAN HELSING *start
for the door.*

VAN HELSING *Yes, see if the Count would like something to drink . . .*

The DOCTORS *exit.*

MAID Is there . . .?

DRACULA Yes, my dear?

MAID Could I get a nice glass of something . . . sherry, perhaps?

DRACULA No, I never drink . . . wine.

DRACULA *moves to the French doors, opening them wide.*

Ahh . . . the night.

MAID Yes, 's quite beautiful, ain't it? Me mum says that the night is
one of the most . . .

DRACULA *stops suddenly, raising a hand toward the* MAID. *The* MAID
stops in mid-sentence and listens.

DRACULA Come to me . . .

She walks toward DRACULA.

You have no will of your own, other than what I command of you.
Do you hear me?

MAID I hear you.

DRACULA When I am gone you will remember none of this. (*Beat.*)
Now, when Doctor Van Helsing orders you to sleep in the room of
your mistress, to watch over her carefully . . . you must do as she
asks. Let no one enter, save myself. Your mistress is threatened
by death, and only I can save her now. Hear me . . .

MAID I understand . . .

DRACULA *moves to her.*

DRACULA Such a sweet young thing, you are . . . you . . .

He leans down toward her neck. It seems as if she is lost, yet DRACULA *only wipes a smudge away from behind her ear.*

   . . . must learn to take better care of yourself.

He laughs to himself and crosses the French doors. He holds them open dramatically, then closes them. He moves quickly to the library door and exits. The MAID *immediately returns to the place in her story.*

MAID   . . . lovely times 'a day. 'Course, it ain't really day, I mean, "night," isn't it?

She looks around, puzzled.

   Count? Count Dracula . . .? (*Beat.*) Rich folks—all the same, ain't they?

Music up as scene shifts to:

A sumptuous library—VAN HELSING *sits on a chair near the divan.* MINA *lies on the couch, looking pale and drawn.* VAN HELSING *holds her wrist, checking her pulse.* ARTHUR *is at his desk, scribbling in a journal.*

ARTHUR "7 September. Richmond. Mina is better now after a bad night. I rejoice for this, for it keeps her mind off the terrible . . ."

VAN HELSING Arthur, come here and have a look . . .

ARTHUR *rises and crosses to the sofa.*

   Look at Miss Mina's beautiful ribbon . . . isn't it lovely?

ARTHUR Yes, it's quite . . .

MINA'*s hand involuntarily goes to it and nervously places along the velvet.*

MINA It was a gift from Lucy. I cherish it dearly, and try to wear it as often as possible.

VAN HELSING So I've noticed . . . (*Beat.*) Arthur.

As if prearranged, ARTHUR *holds* MINA*'s shoulders down while*
VAN HELSING *pulls off the ribbon.* MINA *struggles willfully.*

MINA No! No, I tell you!! How dare you?!! . . .

VAN HELSING Ahh . . . see the marks, Arthur. Again this morning they
are fresh!

ARTHUR But that's impossible . . . my maid slept with her the entire . . .

VAN HELSING *holds* MINA *firmly, staring her directly in the eye.*

VAN HELSING Miss Mina, we do not wish to excite you, but we must
know the truth. How long have you had these marks?

MINA I don't know what you're . . .

VAN HELSING The truth! Your life may depend on it . . .

MINA *finally stops struggling and looks at both doctors, fear spreading*
across her face.

MINA Shortly before Lucy passed away . . .

VAN HELSING *brushes softly at her face, soothing her.*

VAN HELSING My dear, dear girl . . . why didn't you tell us?

MINA I was afraid it would worry you all, for I knew . . . they were the
same as Lucy's.

ARTHUR All the more reason to come forward, Mina.

VAN HELSING Do not fear, Miss Mina . . . for with the truth on our
side, we can surely battle your affliction.

MINA Thank you . . .

VAN HELSING A little pale, perhaps, but we will bring those roses
back to your cheeks.

MINA *hugs* VAN HELSING *tightly, closing her eyes.*

MINA You're so kind to stay on with us, Doctor . . . the great comfort
of a woman here with me is greater than any medication you could
prescribe!

VAN HELSING Thank you, dear child.

She helps MINA *lie back on the divan and slowly checks her eyes, tongue, neck, etc. Throughout the following dialogue.*

Lie back, now . . . relax. Tell me, when did you begin to feel this weakness come upon you?

MINA I suppose . . . two nights after poor Lucy was buried I had . . . bad dreams.

VAN HELSING Tell me about them.

MINA I remember . . . and I thought it strange, but, I was sure I heard the sound of a wolf. Far off. I knew it couldn't be, but . . .

ARTHUR *and* VAN HELSING *secretly look at one another.*

. . . the air was thick. Oppressive. I left the reading lamp near my bed on and opened the windows for a bit of a breeze. When the dreams came, it was as if a cloud . . . no, a mist, perhaps . . . came into my room. (*Beat.*) there, in a haze of my sleep were two red eyes staring at me and . . . teeth. White. Gleaming. Horrible!

ARTHUR There, there . . . (*Beat.*) Doctor, must she . . .?

VAN HELSING Just a but more. (*To* MINA.) Have these dreams persisted?

MINA I'm afraid so . . . every night since then. The red eyes and that terrifying face. (*Beat.*) Also . . . no, you'll laugh at me . . .

VAN HELSING *shakes her head seriously.*

VAN HELSING We are not likely to find much of your story comical, my dear.

MINA No, I suppose not . . . it's just that . . . I was repulsed, of course, in my dream by this creature, and yet, somehow . . . I feel as if I've known it. Almost expected it. For years . . .

ARTHUR How very strange . . .

VAN HELSING Indeed.

ARTHUR No, I mean . . . that she'd say just that. Lucy said much

the same thing, to me. In passing, one day. About "expecting"
all this . . .

MINA My dear Lord . . . I'm lost!

She buries her head in the divan, weeping. The DOCTORS *try valiantly
to comfort her.*

ARTHUR I didn't mean to suggest . . . Oh, Mina . . . please . . .

VAN HELSING Do not fear, Mina . . . come, you must rest . . .

ARTHUR *goes to his desk and rings a bell. After a moment, the* MAID *enters.*

MAID Y'sir?

ARTHUR Please escort Miss Mina to her room, and you will remain
by her side the rest of the day. Is that understood?

MAID Perfectly clear, sir.

ARTHUR Do no leave her for a moment's time!

MAID Y'sir . . . just like last night, sir.

ARTHUR No, apparently not like last night, young lady . . .

VAN HELSING *waves* ARTHUR *off.*

. . . well, just see that you don't.

MAID Y'sir. Thank ye, sir.

She moves to MINA *and wraps the blanket around her shoulders as
she leads her off.* VAN HELSING *signals for* ARTHUR *to come close.*

VAN HELSING Do not be so harsh with the young girl, Arthur.

ARTHUR Well, as you said yourself, the marks on Mina's neck are . . .

VAN HELSING Yes. But this may, I fear, have little to do any longer
with merely staying awake. (*Beat.*) Now it may be simply about
staying alive . . .

Music up as scene shifts to: a bare cell— JONATHAN *sits on a rough
bench, reading a telegram.*

JONATHAN "8 September. London. Have items you requested. Stop.

Am forwarding invoice and log of the 'Demeter' at once. Stop. Hope all's well with your dear fiancée. Stop. Yours, Mr. Peter Hawkins."

The ATTENDANT *escorts* RENFIELD *into the room.* RENFIELD *stops short, staring at* JONATHAN.

RENFIELD Mother? Is that you . . .?

RENFIELD *bursts into hysterics, then stops immediately. He looks squarely at the* ATTENDANT.

Listen, my good man, we're fine here . . . please go and wait by my carriage. You seem awfully tired . . . Rest yourself. Sup. A fine cigar, perhaps . . .

ATTENDANT You want me 't stay, sir?

JONATHAN No, actually . . . I must talk to William alone.

RENFIELD Is that my name?! "William?" Thought I looked a bit more like a "Charles" . . . perhaps "Victoria." (*Beat.*) I've always thought girls names were more manly. I mean, look at the Queen, after all . . . manly.

ATTENDANT Sure now?

JONATHAN We're fine.

RENFIELD . . . she'd take you apart in a fair fight. That's not very respectful, now, is it?

He slaps himself several times. JONATHAN *shakes his head, but waves the* ATTENDANT *off.*

JONATHAN Now, William . . .

RENFIELD You're probably wondering why I called you here.

JONATHAN William, please. I asked to see you. Now, listen to me . . .

RENFIELD *shrieks loudly, bouncing off the walls a bit.* JONATHAN *stands firm, watching him go at it until* RENFIELD *comes within a few inches of* JONATHAN*'s face. He suddenly stops and whispers.*

RENFIELD   John, my God, help me! I'm completely sane, John,

I don't know what's happening to me, but I'm sane, I swear it!!

JONATHAN *grabs him, shaking his roughly.*

JONATHAN   I knew you were there, William! I knew it!! Good old

Renfield . . .

He pulls RENFIELD *over the bench.*

Now, listen . . .

RENFIELD   Are you hungry at all? I've got a little something to snack

on here somewhere . . .

JONATHAN   No, William, please listen! (*Beat.*) My fiancée, Mina, is

dying, and doctors aren't able to come up with any reason why . . .

RENFIELD   Miss Mina?

JONATHAN   Yes . . . I've traced her illness and that of her friend's

back to the arrival of the ship they found you on. The "Demeter."

Think, William, was there anything on board, anything at all, that

could explain this ghastly sickness?

RENFIELD   Oh no . . . I couldn't . . .

JONATHAN   Damn it, man, lives are at stake! Now . . . you were the

only living thing on board when it reached port. I'm not sure what

cargo she was carrying, but I'll soon know that. What else could it

have been? I mean, my God, the entire crew was . . .

RENFIELD *edges closer to* JONATHAN, *whispering.*

RENFIELD   It was Him . . .

JONATHAN   "Him?" Who was it, William?! Who?!!

RENFIELD *looks around the cell, then leans over to answer. As he does,* DRACULA *rises and hovers in front of his window.* RENFIELD *falls back, screaming. When* JONATHAN *turns and looks,* DRACULA *is gone.*

RENFIELD Master, Master! I said nothing to him!! I am loyal to you, Master!!! Please, please, Master!!!!

The ATTENDANT *enters as* JONATHAN *tries to comfort* RENFIELD. RENFIELD *strikes at* JONATHAN *and dashes madly about the room.*

Get away! Go away, you, go!! Master!!! Leave me in peace!!!! Go!!!!!

The ATTENDANT *drags* JONATHAN *away.*

ATTENDANT Ain't no use when he's like this, g'vnor. He's as loony as I seen, and that's plenty. Come on, just aft to let 'im scream it out . . .

JONATHAN But I must know! . . . Renfield!!

RENFIELD Master, come to me!! (*To* JONATHAN.) Go away, you, go from this place!!!

JONATHAN *is aghast as he exits.* RENFIELD *flies back to the window, screaming into the dark.*

Master!! Come to me, Master!!! Master!!!! . . .

He throws himself sobbing to the floor, crying out "Master" to the darkness beyond.

Music up as scene shifts to:

A sumptuous library—ARTHUR, JONATHAN, *and* VAN HELSING *stand up in the room.* VAN HELSING *and* ARTHUR *listen as* JONATHAN *reads from the log of the "Demeter."*

JONATHAN "Log of the 'Demeter.' Midnight. Tonight I saw it, like a man, tall and thin, and ghastly pale. It was moving toward the hold, and I crept behind it, to give it my knife; but the knife went through it, empty as the air . . ."

VAN HELSING Ahh . . . and you can still believe, Mr. Harker, that there is nothing to fear?

JONATHAN *closes the log, placing it on the desk.*

JONATHAN   No, I don't doubt nothing happened. I mean, after all, the entire crew disappeared!

VAN HELSING   Exactly my point . . .

JONATHAN   Yes, but that doesn't mean some . . . apparition . . . was lurking about. Dripping blood and all the rest . . . After all, they found Renfield on board, just as mad as a hatter. For all we know, he may have done in those men himself . . .

VAN HELSING   Is Mr. Renfield tall and thin . . . if you place a blade through him, would he not bleed? No, I do not believe this explanation . . .

JONATHAN   No, of course not . . .

ARTHUR   Please, we must not fight amongst—

VAN HELSING   No, no . . . I have great interest in hearing Mr. Harker's "singular" views on how and why the laws of science operate!

JONATHAN   Well, it doesn't take a doctor to realize that . . .

ARTHUR   Please stop! (*Beat.*) Now, whatever our personal views are, my friends, we must work together. I beg you . . .

JONATHAN *starts to speak, but holds his tongue.*

VAN HELSING   You are right, Arthur . . .

JONATHAN   . . . yes. Yes, of course. Just a bit edgy, forgive me.

ARTHUR   Very good. Now, is there anything else in that log of yours, John . . . any clue as to what the mate was after?

JONATHAN   Afraid not. (*Beat.*) There is a brief mention as to a shipment of crates, but . . .

VAN HELSING   "Crates?" What is this word, "crates?"

ARTHUR   Boxes . . . large boxes. Wooden.

JONATHAN   Yes, but as to the contents, we remain in the dark. I've yet to receive the bloody invoices! . . .

VAN HELSING We must know this information.

JONATHAN And we will, I assure you, just as soon as Mr. Hawkins . . .

ARTHUR What is it, Doctor? (*Beat.*) Do you think some thing may have been encased in one of these . . .

VAN HELSING Possibly. I think a great many things . . . but we now need more facts . . .

JONATHAN Exactly.

VAN HELSING   . . . and one fact remains constant.

ARTHUR Which is?

VAN HELSING Your Mr. Renfield. I think this man could be our key . . .

ARTHUR *and* JONATHAN *look at* VAN HELSING, *curious.*

ARTHUR Explain.

VAN HELSING Just this. Throughout the past few weeks, this little man toys with us, suggesting that perhaps he know answers where they seemingly are none. And when he escapes . . . through inch-thick bars and down thirty feet of smooth rock, I might add . . . where does he go? (*Beat.*) Carfax.

ARTHUR But surely . . . you can't think Count Dracula . . .?

VAN HELSING When I first heard the name "Dracula," it rang some far off bell . . . so while I was back in Holland, I return to my books to freshen my memory.

ARTHUR And?

VAN HELSING "Dracula" is a famous name, one with a dark history on the continent of Europe . . .

JONATHAN Yes, yes . . .

VAN HELSING   . . . a lineage that has been dead for well over three hundred years.

ARTHUR *and* JONATHAN *look at each other.*

JONATHAN Good God, what're you suggesting now, Doctor, that good Count Dracula is a Vampire?! Ha!!

VAN HELSING No, I am not saying anything of the kind, Mr. Harker, only that I believe he perhaps knows more of this affair than he lets on . . .

VAN HELSING *crosses to the windows, looking out.*

A Vampire . . . if you'll permit me the luxury for a moment, Mr. Harker . . . a Vampire must rest in the soil in which it was buried. It has only the hours of night in which it is free to travel this earth. (*Beat.*) Our Vampire . . .

JONATHAN Arthur, please . . .

VAN HELSING IF one exists at all . . . must be English. It must rest in soil nearby . . .

JONATHAN *starts off toward the door.*

JONATHAN I refuse to be a party to this nonsense . . . I'll be with Mina if I'm needed.

VAN HELSING One moment, Mr. Harker . . . I have a proposition.

JONATHAN Yes?

VAN HELSING Tonight . . . I propose an expedition. To the cemetery.

ARTHUR The cemetery? Whatever for . . .?

VAN HELSING To see if Miss Lucy still lies in her grave . . . (*Beat.*) I wage my life on it that she does not.

JONATHAN This is outrageous! Have you no pity, Doctor, for poor Arthur here?!

ARTHUR *says nothing, looking away.*

VAN HELSING More than you know, my rash friend! If I am wrong about poor Lucy, then I shall beg forgiveness for all my wrongdoings . . . but if by night she walks the world as I am most sure she does

. . . then there is much work to be done. (*Beat.*) Arthur, we MUST know for sure . . .

ARTHUR What kind of woman are you . . .?

VAN HELSING The persistent kind. (*Beat.*) Surely, you've read the stories of late concerning "The Woman in White?"

ARTHUR Of course . . .

VAN HELSING Then in your heart, as I do . . . you are beginning to know the truth.

JONATHAN Arthur, I'm truly sorry for this. (*Beat.*) Van Helsing, I am simply flabbergasted by your . . .

ARTHUR *turns to face* JONATHAN *and* VAN HELSING.

ARTHUR What time shall we meet, Doctor?

JONATHAN Arthur, please don't . . .

ARTHUR I said, "what time?"

VAN HELSING *looks at the two men, then solemnly out the* windows.

VAN HELSING . . . at sunset.

Music up as scene shifts to:

The heath—A pale moon casts long shadows across the countryside.

VAN HELSING *and* JONATHAN *crouching to one side of the path, waiting.* VAN HELSING *is scribbling some rough notes in a pocket journal while* JONATHAN *holds a torch.*

VAN HELSING (*Reading aloud.*) "10 September. Richmond."

JONATHAN *stands quickly, looking off.*

JONATHAN Quiet, Doctor . . . someone's coming.

ARTHUR *comes on, looking visibly upset.*

ARTHUR I'm afraid I cracked open every casket in the place . . . I just can't believe . . .

JONATHAN It's alright, Arthur . . .

He puts a supportive arm around ARTHUR.

I'll be glad when we're past all this . . . sweet Lucy, lost to us, and now Mina . . . caught up in some horrific dreams! I can't imagine what . . .

VAN HELSING You remain unsatisfied, Mr. Harker? Can you believe that there is some other explanation than . . .

JONATHAN I am satisfied that Lucy's body is not in her coffin. But that only proves one thing . . .

VAN HELSING And what is that?

JONATHAN That it is not there.

VAN HELSING Marvelous logic . . . I must write that down. (*Beat.*) And HOW do you account for it not being there?

ARTHUR Umm, perhaps . . . a body snatcher.

JONATHAN Yes, or one of the undertaker's people may have stolen it. Any number of things can explain the . . .

Suddenly, VAN HELSING *grabs the torch from* JONATHAN *and douses it.*

What're you . . .?!

She silences him with a look and motions for the two men to hide themselves a but more. As they do, the figure of LUCY *appears. She looks ravishing and is dressed in flowing white. She crosses near them but does not seem to notice them. She wanders off, finally disappearing from view.*

ARTHUR My God . . . Lucy . . .

JONATHAN Impossible . . .

VAN HELSING No, Mr. Harker, not impossible, as you have just seen. (*Beat.*) All too possible, I am afraid . . .

ARTHUR *starts to follow her.*

ARTHUR Lucy . . . Lucy!

JONATHAN *and* VAN HELSING *restrain him.*

VAN HELSING Stop it, Arthur . . . you must stop or you will surely go
mad! (*Beat.*) She is gone now, gone forever from our world. She
has been made a thing of the night . . . Unclean.

The sound of a wolf can be heard, far in the distance.

JONATHAN But she seemed so . . .

VAN HELSING Just an illusion, to lure in the unsuspecting. (*Beat.*)
Believe me when I say that she no longer exists as we once
knew her . . .

VAN HELSING *starts down the path toward Richmond.*

Come, there is much work to be done.

ARTHUR But what about Lucy? Aren't we going to . . .?

VAN HELSING We can do nothing . . . we are not prepared for the task
tonight. We shall return at tomorrow's twilight.

JONATHAN Just what are you proposing we . . .?

VAN HELSING I will reveal all in time. Now, we must return to the asylum
at once . . . Miss Mina can be left unattended no longer. (*Beat.*)
come! The creature that is responsible for this is now among us . . .

She wheels around, addressing JONATHAN *directly.*

Or do you still feel that my theories are "silly wives' tales?"

JONATHAN *says nothing, clearing his throat uncomfortably.*

JONATHAN I don't know . . . what to think.

ARTHUR My head is spinning.

JONATHAN I just . . . what can we do, Doctor?

VAN HELSING I will tell you what we MUST do, and without haste
. . . we must hunt down our Vampire, my young friends, or all
may be lost.

She waves them on and they start quickly back down the stone path.

Music up as scene shifts to:

*A sumptuous library—*MINA *sits on the divan with* DRACULA *reading aloud.*

MINA "I am so happy that I hardly know how to contain myself! Have now recently met a gentleman here at the estate who frees my soul inside . . . I feel compelled to write down my thoughts. Spent six hours or more with him last night talking about the world beyond England; all manner of literature, philosophy, music and the like. What are these thoughts that I am having?"

MINA *closes the journal she is holding a blushes a bit.*

I'm sorry . . . I feel almost silly reading this to you, Count . . . like a schoolgirl.

DRACULA No, no, it is lovely to hear that my visits are of some use to you. That you might find them . . . how would you say . . . "pleasing."

MINA But I do . . .

DRACULA Careful, Miss Mina, for you shall spoil me with such affection.

He takes MINA'*s hand into his own.*

And what of your Mr. Harker? Your wedding day is . . .?

MINA Well, no date is set as yet . . . but soon, I trust.

DRACULA And you are happy, no?

MINA Of course . . .

She smiles weakly at the COUNT, *then turns away.*

DRACULA I fear, Miss Mina, that you withhold some truth from me.

MINA No . . . I just . . .

DRACULA Rest assured that it will go no further than this room.

MINA Oh, Count Dracula . . . why must you make it so horribly easy to open my heart to you? I feel we're actually communicating when we speak to one another . . .

DRACULA As do I.

MINA . . . and that you look at me as if we equals. That I am your equal, not just a "woman."

DRACULA This, I'm afraid is simply not true, Miss Mina . . . (*Beat.*) for I do see you as a woman. A most lovely carefree woman.

MINA Count Dracula, please . . . I . . .

DRACULA Equal, yes, to be sure . . . yet so different from myself. So refreshing, mysterious . . .

MINA I am . . . so weak . . .

She leans forward, almost in a trance, as if to kiss the COUNT *but he helps her to her feet and escorts her to the window.*

DRACULA Perhaps the night air will revive you . . . (*Beat.*) I find that it always does wonders for me.

MINA Yes.

Together they stand at the window, taking in the night as the sheer curtains billow around them.

DRACULA Ahh . . . there, Mina. Can you feel it, the power of the dark?

MINA Oh yes . . . Count . . .

They begin to kiss deeply.

DRACULA I have loved you, Mina, from the moment we met . . . when my gaze first fell upon you. (*Beat.*) Come to me, be my Queen . . .

She looks at him curiously, not understanding.

MINA But I'm . . . I've pledged myself to . . .

DRACULA It is our destiny, my dear . . . our fate that one day we
would . . .

They continue to kiss as the door to the library swings open. VAN HELS-
ING, ARTHUR, *and* JONATHAN *enter.* MINA *walks out from behind the curtains to greet them. She looks back uncomfortably to the* COUNT, *but
he has vanished. She says nothing of this to the others.*

JONATHAN Darling Mina . . . you'll catch a death of cold standing
near the window like that! Come away at once . . .

MINA John, John . . . hold me . . .

She runs to him, burying herself in his arms.

JONATHAN Silly child . . . (*Beat.*) For all your talk of progress and
womanly nonsense, you still need your man to feel safe, don't you?

MINA I don't know . . . I don't know . . .

ARTHUR *and* VAN HELSING *move toward the window, pulling the curtains
closed after looking out briefly.*

ARTHUR She's as white as fresh linen . . .

VAN HELSING Yes. I believe she's just had a terrible fright. But from
what?

She crosses to MINA.

(*To* MINA.) My dear, you are still too weak to be up and about alone
. . . you must take care if we are to win back your health.

MINA I'm sorry, I just . . .

VAN HELSING What is it?

MINA Nothing, I'm fine, really . . .

JONATHAN *holds her more tightly.*

JONATHAN Come now, up to bed . . . I'll tuck you in. There's a good
girl. (*To the others.*) If you'll excuse us . . .

He leads the weakened MINA *toward the door. She looks back lingeringly at the windows, then exits.* VAN HELSING *watches her intently, then crosses to the couch, feeling both cushions.*

VAN HELSING Our Mina was not alone in this room before we arrived . . . I can feel it.

ARTHUR But there's no one here now . . .

VAN HELSING No. Not now . . .

ARTHUR . . . and we came through the only door leading into the room.

VAN HELSING Yes. (*Beat.*) And it was not the maid, for she was downstairs when we arrived.

ARTHUR True. So what makes you think . . .?

VAN HELSING Just the feeling of this place as we walked in . . . I felt the same tonight. On the heath.

ARTHUR *considers this for a moment.*

ARTHUR She did seem shaken, you're right about that . . . almost as if she'd seen a ghost.

ARTHUR *exits, leaving* VAN HELSING *alone.*

VAN HELSING Perhaps she has, my boy . . . perhaps she has.

Music up as scene shifts to:

*A sumptuous library—*ARTHUR *sits at his desk, reading from his journal.*

ARTHUR "12 September. Vexed by the creature, with little information in our favor. We know It exists and the horrible deeds It is capable of committing . . . but who or what can It be? What weighs most heavy on my mind, however, is Lucy. I do not know how I can possibly survive the duty we must face tonight."

VAN HELSING *enters.*

VAN HELSING Are you alright, my boy?

ARTHUR Yes, yes. I just find that I now dread the coming of night-fall. (*Beat.*) It's funny, I used to so love the shadows and silence of the evenings here in Richmond . . . taking long strolls by the river with my . . . Lucy . . .

VAN HELSING Dear, dear boy . . . this has been so horrible for you. And still it is not over . . .

ARTHUR I'll be alright.

VAN HELSING And tonight . . . will you be strong enough for that, as well?

ARTHUR . . . yes.

VAN HELSING If you are not, then I am afraid your Lucy may be damned to walk the earth for eternity.

ARTHUR Do not fear . . . when the time comes, I shall do what I must.

JONATHAN *bursts through the door to the library, carrying a sheath of papers.*

JONATHAN Arthur! Doctor Van Helsing! It's come . . . I've got it!!

ARTHUR What is it, Jonathan?

JONATHAN The invoices, the original manifest of the "Demeter!"

VAN HELSING Marvelous! Now we may have some idea of what dangers lie in . . .

JONATHAN Yes . . . I haven't had time to look over the . . .

ARTHUR Spread them out over here, John . . .

VAN HELSING Yes, here. Bring them here and we shall . . .

The MAID *suddenly enters the room, calling* ARTHUR.

MAID Beggin' off, sir, but Miss Mina's in a terrible state!

ARTHUR What is it, girl . . . what's the matter?

MAID She's got out of her bed and is trying to get downstairs . . . woke in a 'orrible sweat, she did, and clawing at 'erself, too.

ARTHUR I've told you, you mustn't leave her for a moment!

MAID I've locked 'er in 'er room, bolted shut . . . but I don't think I can watch 'er myself. 'S like she's got the strength a' ten men! . . .

JONATHAN What?!

MAID Yes sir, and she keeps yelling out fer Miss Lucy . . . saying she can see 'er out 'er window. Saying they must be with "'im" (*Beat.*) No idea who "'im" is though . . .

VAN HELSING Hurry, you must go to her! Understand that you cannot, whatever she says to you, tries to charm you with . . . you cannot let her leave this house tonight!

ARTHUR Come on, John, I'll give her something to make her sleep . . . I'll need you for this!

JONATHAN Right behind you, Arthur!

JONATHAN *drops the invoices on a nearby desk as he and* ARTHUR *race for the door.* VAN HELSING *watches them go, then crosses to the papers that* JONATHAN *has left. She begins to scan them rapidly, finally stopping on a single entry.*

VAN HELSING . . . my God. (*Reading.*) "Five wooden containers of earth. Potting soil. (*Beat.*) Delivery care of . . . Carfax Abbey. Invoice billing to Count . . .

DRACULA *has appeared behind* VAN HELSING *out of thin air.*

DRACULA Doctor Van Helsing, we meet again . . .

VAN HELSING *spins about, audibly gasping.*

VAN HELSING Dracula.

DRACULA Yes.

VAN HELSING I didn't hear you . . .

DRACULA . . . slip in? No. Your carpets here are so thick, and my step a quiet one. Forgive me if I frighten you . . .

VAN HELSING No, I'm just . . . you see . . .

She tries to hide the papers behind her, but she moves away as DRACULA *approaches. He picks up a sheet from the pile, studying it.*

DRACULA Why can no one ever spell my name correctly? (*Beat.*) There is no "K" in "Dracula." Ahh, well, no matter.

In a flash, the paper goes up in a burst of flame and smoke.

Oh no, a most unfortunate accident! I hope you did not need this . . . How can I repay you?

VAN HELSING No need . . . I have all the information from it that I require.

DRACULA Indeed?

VAN HELSING, *trying to remain calm, begins to question* DRACULA.

VAN HELSING Tell me, Count, I am curious . . . are you of the Voivode Dracula line?

DRACULA Why, yes. You know of my heritage? (*Picking up a book from the desk.*) Ah, you have been reading up on me. I am flattered . . .

VAN HELSING Only what I can recall from history books, bits of information picked up in the wilds or Europe . . . I seem to remember a "Vlad the Impaler" who dispatched his enemies by skewering them on a sharpened stake . . .

DRACULA Yes, a great uncle, I believe . . . and honored in my country as a valiant war hero.

VAN HELSING "Dracula . . . Dracula . . ."

DRACULA Yes. With no "K . . ."

VAN HELSING Knowing a bit of your native tongue, this translates to . . . ?

DRACULA "The Dragon."

VAN HELSING I see. (*Beat.*) My translation comes from an older
source . . .

DRACULA Really?

VAN HELSING . . . meaning "The Devil."

DRACULA Hmm. Interesting.

VAN HELSING . . . yet no references listed in any of my sources. Not
in the last few years. (*Beat.*) Say, three hundred years . . .

DRACULA And yet here I stand before you, my dear Doctor. Now,
how can this be explained?

VAN HELSING . . . I don't know.

DRACULA I'm afraid it cannot be . . . what is, my dear, simply IS.
(*Beat.*) And how is our fair patient, Miss Mina?

VAN HELSING She progresses slowly . . .

DRACULA Ahh. This is most distressing news.

VAN HELSING Although just tonight I had discovered a prescription
which may save her . . . (*Beat.*) Would you care to see, Count?

DRACULA Please. Anything you prescribe for Miss Mina has the
greatest interest for me.

DRACULA *follows* VAN HELSING *to the desk. As she rummages through
a drawer,* DRACULA *begins to loom over her. She waits for the last
moment, then wheels about, a large crucifix in one hand.* DRACULA
staggers back as the doctor confidently moves toward him.

DRACULA *folds into himself as* VAN HELSING *keeps up the pressure;
at the last moment* DRACULA *looks up at* VAN HELSING, *pathetic and
withered. Then, without warning, he smiles and his head snaps to
attention.*

Boo!

He stands instantly and without difficulty, pointing to VAN HELSING*'s
crucifix for effect.*

My dear Doctor . . . Haven't you people hidden behind the symbols of your God for enough centuries . . .?

VAN HELSING *bravely tries to hang on, with* DRACULA *coming to her side and taking a look at the cross. He grabs* VAN HELSING*'s hand and turns it slowly until she must drop the crucifix. He then brings her hand to his mouth and turns it slightly; he gives it an affectionate kiss as he caresses it. Finally,* VAN HELSING *pulls herself free and backs away.*

VAN HELSING So . . .

DRACULA Yes . . .

VAN HELSING It is you . . . You are the Prince of Darkness.

A storm can be heard rumbling in the distance. Flash of lightning, crash of thunder.

DRACULA You are so wise, my dear Doctor . . . for one who has yet to live even one lifetime.

VAN HELSING You shall not have Miss Mina, this I promise you.

DRACULA Do not make promises you may not live to keep . . .

DRACULA *backs* VAN HELSING *into a corner, towering over her.*

I could kill you right now . . . all of you. Except my Queen, my Mina.

VAN HELSING If she is to die, I will put a stake through her myself . . . and in the daylight, so that her soul may rest in peace!

DRACULA So much knowledge . . . so sure that good will triumph over evil. (*Beat.*) But you must know, Doctor, in your heart, that evil will remain the mistress of this world long after you and yes, even I, have become nothing but dust . . .

VAN HELSING No . . . it mustn't.

DRACULA If you were truly wise, Doctor, you would return to your native country, now that you have learned what you have learned . . .

VAN HELSING Not until you, and those like you, have been destroyed . . . to this I am pledged.

DRACULA *smiles and moves toward* VAN HELSING.

DRACULA Perhaps it is time for you to die . . .

VAN HELSING *tries to look away but* DRACULA *raises a hand, pulling her toward him. She crosses the space between them slowly, fighting his power at every turn.*

Your will is strong. (*Beat.*) Come to me . . .

VAN HELSING Yes.

As she reaches DRACULA *he begins to pull her close to him. She pulls wolfsbane from a jacket pocket and presses it to his face. He reacts violently, turning away and tearing at his face.*

Flash of lightning, crash of thunder.

DRACULA AAAHHH!!

VAN HELSING In this my faith need not be so strong, Count . . .

DRACULA *points a wary finger at the* DOCTOR, *his face twisted in rage. Suddenly, there is a pounding on the library door.*

DRACULA Wolfsbane!

ARTHUR (*Offstage.*) Doctor! Doctor Van Helsing . . . open the door!

DRACULA Listen to me and take heed, Doctor Van Helsing . . . in the past five hundred years, all those who would have stopped me have died violent deaths. I swear you shall join them!

Flash of lightning, crash of thunder. The lights in the room go out. There is more pounding on the door and ARTHUR *enters, carrying a lighted candle in one hand.*

ARTHUR The door is jammed . . . are you alright, Doctor?

VAN HELSING, *weakened from her duel with* DRACULA, *sits in a chair.*

VAN HELSING Quite. (*Beat.*) Is Mina . . .?

ARTHUR *nods slowly.*

ARTHUR In an awful state, I'm afraid . . . eyes on fire and ready to leap from her bedroom window. She swears that Lucy is alive . . .

VAN HELSING She must never know the truth. We cannot allow it!

ARTHUR . . . no. (*Beat.*) I've gotten her to drink an elixir that should bring on sleep. Jonathan is with her now, and the maid is preparing a bed in the same room.

VAN HELSING Ask the attendant to post himself outside the door as well . . . we will need Jonathan for our dark duties tonight.

ARTHUR Yes. Of course . . .

ARTHUR *looks about the room.*

You know, it's strange, but when I couldn't get the door open a few minutes ago, I would've sworn . . . I thought I heard voices.

VAN HELSING You were not imagining it. Count Dracula was here . . .

ARTHUR What? But that's . . . where did he go? I was just outside, and no one's gone out . . .

VAN HELSING I'm afraid our Count has no need for the doors and windows of this world.

ARTHUR What do you mean by . . .?

VAN HELSING Dracula is our Vampire. (*Beat.*) Come, this cannot be a complete surprise to you, Arthur . . .

ARTHUR Yes . . . I mean, no . . . I thought him mysterious, but . . . (*Beat.*) How can you be sure?!

VAN HELSING Of this I had my suspicions from the beginning, but now, I KNOW.

ARTHUR But surely, Doctor, there must be some . . .

VAN HELSING Mistake? Oh no, believe me, Arthur, the evil we seek is at Carfax Abbey. The Count admitted to it all. Sure that he would kill me . . .

ARTHUR My God . . .

Flash of lightning, crash of thunder.

VAN HELSING The shipment of crates on the "Demeter" was directed
to Carfax, paid for by Dracula himself . . . and each box contained
soil from Transylvania.

ARTHUR Brought here by the "Demeter?" (*Beat.*) But . . . that would
mean . . .

VAN HELSING Yes. Our Mr. Renfield must surely be in league with
this devil in some way . . .

ARTHUR My Lord, Doctor, what can we . . .?

VAN HELSING No, this may be a positive thing. We may be able to
use Renfield to our advantage here. A plan is forming in my . . .
(*Beat.*) But first we must hurry to Miss Lucy's tomb.

ARTHUR Oh. Yes . . .

VAN HELSING Courage, my boy. If you loved her as you professed,
then you will surely be able to do what you must for her eternal
salvation.

Flash of lightning, crash of thunder.

It will be morning soon. Gather your things and find Mr. Harker . . .
now that Dracula is aware of our plans, we must move swiftly to
defeat him. (*Beat.*) If we do not, I fear none of us may live to see
another dawn.

Music up as scene shifts to:

The entrance to a tomb—Flash of lightning, crash of thunder.
JONATHAN *stands nearby, tired and cold. He reads loud from his
journal.*

JONATHAN "Am now convinced of the horrors we face . . . seeing
Mina in such a state this night has finally opened my eyes. So it
is Dracula, and he means to have my Mina for his Queen! I have

yet to even meet this man, but I know that I will stop him with my final breath, if I must. Even the word "Dracula" makes Mina's eyes fill with desire . . . I now feel as though I'm dying inside and our duty tonight leaves me colder still.

VAN HELSING and ARTHUR appear with torches up the stone path that leads to the crypt. JONATHAN closes his journal, quizzing them. ARTHUR carries a savage looking stake and large wooden mallet in one hand.

Anything?

ARTHUR Afraid not, old man, it is just as before. Her coffin lies thrown open and she's . . . she's . . .

VAN HELSING She is the "Woman in White" of which the papers write their stories on . . .

They are silent for a moment, looking at one another and feeling the magnitude of what they now face.

JONATHAN Look. Nearly daybreak . . .

VAN HELSING Yes, it was about this time last night that she returned.

The two men look at her, admiring her bravery.

ARTHUR You came back here . . . ALONE? This past morning?

VAN HELSING Of course. I knew that we must be certain that is was to here that she comes each dawn . . .

JONATHAN I believe I . . . owe you an apology, of sorts, Doctor. For everything . . .

VAN HELSING Nonsense.

ARTHUR It's all just so . . . beyond me. I can't . . .

Suddenly, LUCY appears in flowing white. She moves across the stage toward them, aware but not fearful. Blood trickles from her mouth.

LUCY Arthur . . .

ARTHUR My God . . . Lucy.

JONATHAN (*To* VAN HELSING.) Look at her mouth . . .

VAN HELSING . . . yes.

LUCY My own sweet Arthur . . .

ARTHUR How beautiful you look . . .

LUCY Come to me, Arthur . . .

ARTHUR *takes a step toward her, but is restrained by* JONATHAN *and* VAN HELSING. LUCY *smiles at them, passing by on her way toward the waiting coffin.*

ARTHUR Lucy! (*To the others.*) Let me go!!

JONATHAN No, Arthur!

ARTHUR Please, she's not dead . . . she's not dead!!

VAN HELSING Look at her, Arthur . . . see her with your own eyes!!

LUCY I long for you, Arthur . . . Come be with me, my darling. It's lonely without you . . .

She reaches out toward ARTHUR, *who struggles violently to free himself.* VAN HELSING *points to the sky above.*

VAN HELSING It is too late . . . look, Miss Lucy, the dawn!

LUCY *shrieks like a caged animal, forcing her way past the men and along the path toward the tomb.* ARTHUR *drops the hammer and starts to follow but is grabbed by* VAN HELSING *and* JONATHAN. VAN HELSING *picks up the instrument and places it firmly in* ARTHUR'*s hand.*

ARTHUR No . . .

VAN HELSING Yes!

JONATHAN He can't do it . . .

VAN HELSING He must do it! (*Shaking* ARTHUR.) You must!! Only you can set her free!!!

ARTHUR But she's . . . she's . . .

VAN HELSING You must free her soul or you will never forgive yourself, my boy . . . (*Pushing him.*) Now go!!

ARTHUR *gathers his strength and starts off down the path, alone.*
VAN HELSING *and* JONATHAN *wait anxiously near the entrance.*

And still it will not be over . . . we must find the five boxes of earth
that Dracula is dependant on. We must desecrate them with Holy
Water and then we must track him down and destroy him . . .

JONATHAN   He'll return for Mina tonight, won't he? I can feel it . . .

VAN HELSING   Yes. Yes, I'm afraid he will . . . (*Beat.*) And we must be
ready for him . . .

Both VAN HELSING *and* JONATHAN *turn quickly and react to the horrid
sound of a hammer striking wood.* LUCY*'s screams can be heard
erupting from the tomb and lifting off into the sky.*

Music up as scene shifts to:

*A sumptuous library—*MINA *sits on the divan, writing in her journal.
The* MAID *sits nearby at one of the small writing tables, nervously
watching* MINA.

MINA   "13 September. Richmond. It is strange to be kept in the dark
as I am these days, although I am secretly thankful for it . . . I feel
that I am no longer in control of my feelings or emotions. I grow
weaker each day and the dream persists . . . Count Dracula haunts
my every thought. What is happening?!"

MAID   'scuse me, mum, would you be caring for any dinner this
evening?

MINA   No, that's quite alright, dear.

MAID   As you wish . . .

They return to silence for a moment, then the door swings open.
VAN HELSING, ARTHUR *and* JONATHAN *enter the room, covered in filth and
obviously weary.* JONATHAN *carries the hammer and several stakes.*

Oh look, sirs, you're back . . . but you're all dirty, from head to toe!

ARTHUR There's a good girl, run and have Mr. Renfield brought to us here . . .

MAID Y'sir.

ARTHUR . . . and be sure to relay that he must be unshackled.

MAID . . . y'sir.

The MAID *exits the room quickly.* VAN HELSING *has sat in a chair and* JONATHAN *has crossed to* MINA.

JONATHAN Hello, my love . . .

MINA Hello, Jonathan.

JONATHAN Any better?

MINA A bit. (*Beat.*) So, what have you all been . . .?

JONATHAN We've just finished off the good Count's . . .

VAN HELSING *motions for* JONATHAN *to be silent.*

MINA What? (*Beat.*) Jonathan, what have you three been up to, and why do you have those horrible-looking . . .?

VAN HELSING Do not worry yourself, Miss Mina.

MINA Yes, but . . .

VAN HELSING You must not let yourself become too worked up. Your health demands that you rest now . . . (*Beat.*) Arthur and I must arrange several things before my departure . . .

MINA Oh, you're leaving us, Doctor Van Helsing?

VAN HELSING Soon. My work here is nearly finished . . .

MINA I see. (*Beat.*) Does that mean me? Am I . . .?

VAN HELSING Oh no, Miss Murray, you shall live to be old and gray, a mother of many children, I imagine. (*Beat.*) If all goes well, you could marry as early as All Hallow's Eve. Perhaps sooner . . .

MINA Really? I am so grateful . . .

ARTHUR Now rest. We shall return in a few moments' time . . .

VAN HELSING *rises and starts off, passing* JONATHAN *as she goes.*

VAN HELSING (*To* JONATHAN.) Tell her nothing that will raise her
suspicions, Mr. Harker. Until we can finish off Dracula, I'm afraid
she is his . . .

JONATHAN I understand.

VAN HELSING *and* ARTHUR *exit.* JONATHAN *wanders about the room, trying
not to look at* MINA.

MINA Come, John . . . sit by my side and hold me.

JONATHAN Yes, alright.

*He goes to her and sits, setting the hammer and stakes on the
ground beside the divan.*

MINA Ahh, look . . . it'll be evening soon! (*Beat.*) How can anyone
like the daylight? I find it's night now when I feel most alive . . .
alive to enjoy life, and love. Our life.

She looks deep into his eyes.

Kiss me, Jonathan . . . I need your touch.

JONATHAN I don't know if that's . . .

MINA Kiss me.

JONATHAN *moves to peck her on the cheek but is engulfed in a
passionate embrace. He feels* MINA *slowly moving towards his neck
and he quickly pulls away, standing.*

Do I repulse you so, John? Now it is you that seems distant and
cold.

JONATHAN No, I just . . . umm . . .

MINA I won't bite, promise . . . (*Beat.*) Jonathan, you must tell me
what you've been doing all day.

He shakes his head firmly.

JONATHAN I can't. You wouldn't understand . . .

MINA As a woman? Is that what you mean . . .?

JONATHAN Nothing so simple, I'm afraid . . .

MINA Then what?

JONATHAN No, the Doctor's forbidden me from . . .

MINA You say you love me, yet you don't trust me.

JONATHAN I trust you with my life, Mina. It's just that . . .

MINA He knows everything . . .

JONATHAN *looks up, shocked.*

JONATHAN Mina . . .

MINA Oh, Jonathan . . . I know the Count is responsible for this!
(*Beat.*) Promise me that you will tell me nothing of the plans
you've formed . . . I don't know what's happening to me!

JONATHAN *tries to hold her but she pushes him away.*

While this scar remains at my throat . . . I know I am not yours.

JONATHAN Don't say that . . .

MINA He knows what we think, what we feel . . . he knows everything.
(*Beat.*) If you do not stop him tonight . . . I will be his on the morrow.
Free me, John!

JONATHAN You shall be, after tonight. I promise . . .

*He grabs her suddenly and kisses her deeply. She melts in his arms.
He then stands, scooping up several of the stakes and the mallet.*

MINA Hurry, my love . . . it is nearly dusk.

JONATHAN *moves quickly out of the room as* VAN HELSING *and* ARTHUR
appear at the door. JONATHAN *motions them to follow without a
word as the* MAID *and the* ATTENDANT *enter the room and sit, watching*
MINA *closely.*

Please hurry . . .

Music up as scene shifts to:

A tomb—on a set of high stairs comes the light of several torches.

A sound is heard, feet scampering in the dark that finally stop when voices begin.

JONATHAN This way!

ARTHUR These tunnels go down forever . . .

VAN HELSING Yes, it is no wonder we did not originally find this passage . . .

ARTHUR But thankfully we've destroyed four of his five coffins already . . . now we MUST find the fifth.

VAN HELSING True. If we do not, I fear he will go into hiding . . . wait a hundred years or more, until we are but ash and dust, and then he will come to claim Mina for his own.

JONATHAN Hidden behind the bookcase! How ingenious . . .

ARTHUR We can thank Renfield for that when we find him . . .

VAN HELSING If we find him . . . it was a brilliant plan to let him escape, to lead us to Dracula's lair. But we must reach the Count before Renfield can warn him . . . or, heaven forbid, before Dracula rises on his own.

More movement in the dark.

ARTHUR There, I heard something!

JONATHAN Yes, down those stairs . . . come on!!

RENFIELD *scampers into view, wide eyed and running.*

RENFIELD Master . . . Master, I'm coming!

JONATHAN It's Renfield's voice . . .

VAN HELSING We must catch him!!

ARTHUR This way!!

RENFIELD *moves onto the stage and over to a huge, ominous casket.* RENFIELD *begins clawing at the top.*

RENFIELD Master, Master . . . come out! They've tricked me. Oh, how clever they are, so clever . . . let me escape they did!!

Nothing from the coffin. RENFIELD *sits down and begins to weep.*

Oh Master . . . Master . . .

The lid to the coffin snaps open and DRACULA *sits up, eyes red with hate.*

DRACULA Ahh, sunset!!

RENFIELD Master, I didn't do it . . . I said nothing! They followed me here, it's not my fault!!! Don't hurt me . . .

DRACULA Did I not promise you that you will come to me at your death to enjoy eternal life? To hold the power of life over the bodies and souls of others?

RENFIELD Yes, Master! I want it . . . I want that!!

DRACULA . . . and you shall have it!

Still sitting in his casket, DRACULA *seizes* RENFIELD *by the face and lifts him off the ground. He nearly turns the smaller man's head in a circle as the sound of his neck snapping is heard.* RENFIELD *falls lifelessly to the ground.*

RENFIELD Master . . .

VAN HELSING, ARTHUR *and* JONATHAN *appear on the steps at the same moment.* DRACULA *smiles at them.*

DRACULA Ahh, gentlemen . . . I love it when friends drop over.

VAN HELSING Count Dracula, your life in death has reached its end . . .

DRACULA I doubt that very much . . .

JONATHAN come out of there, Count . . . come out where I can get at you!

DRACULA Mr. Harker, I presume . . . my rival.

JONATHAN How dare you?!

DRACULA You fools, you think you can destroy me?

ARTHUR   Your coffins have been destroyed, Count, and my Lucy's
soul safely put to rest . . .

JONATHAN   Now it's your turn.

DRACULA   You are a most jealous suitor, Mr. Harker.

The small group begins to advance on DRACULA, *but he stops them
with a word.*

Stop where you are! You would challenge me?! You, with your
pale faces all in a row, like sheep to a butcher . . . you shall be
sorry yet. My revenge has just begun!! Mr. Harker, the woman
you love is mine already, and through her, you and the others
shall yet to be mine . . .

VAN HELSING   We must stop him now . . . before he is strong enough
to rise!

JONATHAN *moves forward.*

Should you escape Dracula, we now know how to save Mina's
soul, if not her life . . .

DRACULA   Ah yes, the stake . . . but only if she dies by day.

VAN HELSING   Exactly.

DRACULA   Then I shall see that she perishes by night . . . this night.

JONATHAN   You!! . . .

VAN HELSING   Careful, Mr. Harker . . . he know he is doomed. This
is his only revenge, to trouble our dreams . . .

JONATHAN *continues to advance on* DRACULA.

DRACULA   I shall put Mina above all others, Mr. Harker, rest assured
of that . . . but I have many other wives. Many. See for yourself! . . .

The WIVES *appear on the stairs behind them, snarling and horrible, with
wild hair hanging in their faces and wide mouths filled with gnashing
teeth.* DRACULA *snaps the lid on the coffin back down disappearing
from view.*

VAN HELSING Quick, Jonathan . . . open the coffin! We shall hold them off with our torches! (*To the* WIVES.) Back, back!!

ARTHUR For God's sake, man, hurry!!

JONATHAN *runs to the casket, throwing it open. It is empty.*

JONATHAN He's gone!

ARTHUR What?!

JONATHAN The devil's disappeared!!

VAN HELSING My God . . . he escaped us!!!

VAN HELSING *and* ARTHUR *wave torches at the approaching* WIVES. JONATHAN *starts to join the group, but stops at the crumpled body of* RENFIELD. *He kneels and holds his friend for a moment.*

JONATHAN Poor Renfield . . . sleep, my friend, your battle is over.

VAN HELSING *looks back at* JONATHAN, *gesturing with a free hand.*

VAN HELSING Come, we've left Miss Mina alone . . . alone with that thing!! We must return to the asylum!!

JONATHAN *joins the others as they slowly fight their way back up the stairs as the* WIVES *give up each inch of the way with screams and hissing. After a moment, they all disappear from view.*

Suddenly, the casket lid snaps open and out steps DRACULA. *He lets out a blood-curdling laugh and then disappears in a puff of smoke.*

Music up as scene shifts to:

A sumptuous library— MINA *lies sleeping on the divan. Suddenly,* DRACULA *appears at the window, moving to her. As he passes the* MAID *and* ATTENDANT, *he waves a hand over each and they fall asleep.* DRACULA *reaches the sofa and kneels at the feet of* MINA.

DRACULA My Queen . . .

MINA . . . Count?

DRACULA I have come for you. It is time . . .

MINA Yes.

DRACULA Rule with me . . .

MINA I . . . I . . . will, but first . . .

DRACULA Come, my dear . . .

MINA A kiss . . . first a kiss as I leave this world . . .

DRACULA Mina. (*Beat.*) How I love thee . . .

DRACULA *pulls her to his mouth and they kiss hungrily. Slowly,* MINA *raises a hand that has been hidden from view and, with surprising speed, drives home one of the stakes* JONATHAN *has left behind.* DRACULA *recoils and stares at her.*

Mina . . .?

She pulls the COUNT *close again, kissing him deeply as his life ebbs away. After a moment, he lies lifeless in her lap as she begins to weep.* VAN HELSING, JONATHAN *and* ARTHUR *burst into the room but stop at the sight. They stay at a respectful distance, lowering their heads.*

MINA Rest now, my love . . . you've finally come to rest.

She looks up and out—a smile slowly growing on her face.

MINA Arthur has given me a little opiate of some kind, as I had not slept well the night before. I have taken it, and am now waiting for sleep once more . . . I hope I have not done wrong, for as sleep begins to flirt with me, a new fear comes. That I may have deprived myself of the power of waking. For although I eat and read and walk the grounds of Richmond, I feel somewhat strange. I feel, in fact, as though I may never wake again . . .

Music up as lights fade slowly to:

Silence. Darkness.

END OF PLAY

New York. Middle of the night. Now.

Meet Beth and Doug: two people who have no problem getting dates with their partners of choice. What they do have is an awkward encounter after spending one hit night together following a drunken wedding reception.

Slyly profound and irresistibly passionate, *The Way We Get By* is Neil LaBute's audacious tale of a very modern romance—a sharp, sexy, fresh look at love and lust and the whole damn thing.

$14.95 978-1-4683-1208-9

In the companion piece to Neil LaBute's 2009 Tony-nominated *Reasons to be Pretty*, Greg, Steph, Carly, and Kent pick up their lives three years later, but in different romantic pairings, as they each search desperately for that elusive object of desire: happiness.

"Mr. LaBute is more relaxed as a playwright than he's ever been. He is clearly having a good time revisiting old friends . . . you're likely to feel the same way . . . the most winning romantic comedy of the summer, replete with love talk, LaBute-style, which isn't so far from hate talk . . . "   —**Ben Brantley, *New York Times***

$14.95 978-1-4683-0721-4

THE OVERLOOK PRESS • NEW YORK • WWW.OVERLOOKPRESS.COM

With *Reasons to be Pretty Happy*, Neil LaBute revisits the characters first introduced in *Reasons to be Pretty* (2009 Tony Award-nominated Best Play) and *Reasons to be Happy* as they grapple with that eternal question: Have I become the person I wanted to be?

In this essential new American play, which concludes his brilliant and penetrating "Reasons" trilogy, Neil LaBute, with perfect clarity and enormous heart, captures and refracts the moment in these characters' lives—and in our own as well—when they finally land on a "pretty good" version of happiness. *Reasons to be Pretty Happy* had its world premiere at MCC Theater in a benefit reading that featured Paul Rudd, Amber Tamblyn, Jennifer Mudge, and Norbert Leo Butz and was directed by Neil LaBute.

$14.95 978-1-4683-1708-4

In *How To Fight Loneliness,* Neil LaBute's affecting, humane, and boldly provocative new play, Jodie, a young wife, and her husband, Brad, seek out Tate, an old school mate, to help them out with something they can't quite manage themselves. This timely, dark, and dazzling play takes a penetrating, point-blank look three people crossing the slipperiest of moral terrains as they test their true capacity for facing loneliness.

$14.95   978-1-4683-1604-9

THE OVERLOOK PRESS · NEW YORK · WWW.OVERLOOKPRESS.COM